PLAZA

THE LIVING WAGE

THE LIVING
WAGE

BUILDING A FAIR ECONOMY

R O B E R T   P O L L I N   A N D
S T E P H A N I E   L U C E

THE NEW PRESS   NEW YORK
1998

Library of Congress Cataloging-in-Publication Data

Pollin, Robert.
   The living wage : building a fair economy / Robert Pollin
and Stephanie Luce.
      p.   cm.
   Includes bibliographical references and index.
   ISBN 1-56584-409-2
   1. Minimum wage— United States.   2. Cost and standard of living—
United States.   3. Working class—United States.   I. Luce,
Stephanie.   II. Title.
HD4918.P65   1998
331.2'3—dc21   98-11110
                                                     CIP

            Published by The New Press, New York
       Distributed by W. W. Norton & Company, Inc., New York

The New Press was established in 1990 as a not-for-profit alternative to
the large, commercial publishing houses currently dominating the
book industry. The New Press operates in the public interest rather
than for private gain, and is committed to publishing, in innovative
ways, works of educational, cultural, and community value that might
not be considered sufficiently profitable. PHONE # ANSWERS

PRINTED IN THE UNITED STATES OF AMERICA NORTON

9 8 7 6 5 4 3 2 1

To the Los Angeles Living Wage Coalition
and its director, Madeline Janis-Aparicio

for their commitment to economic justice
and their achievements toward making
it a reality

—Contents

—List of Figures

—List of Tables

—Preface and Acknowledgments

Books on economic policy are almost always products of an ongoing debate in society. In this case, the link between debate and book could not be stronger—the connection, as Antonio Gramsci would say, is "organic."

The project began in August 1996, when Madeline Janis-Aparicio, the leader of the Los Angeles Living Wage Coalition, visited Bob Pollin at his office at the University of California–Riverside economics department. She asked whether he would provide a professional assessment of the living wage proposal being considered by the Los Angeles City Council. The coalition approached Bob because they were told he would be sympathetic to the idea. In fact, he was. However, he also made clear to Madeline that he had not carefully followed developments in the living wage movement. As such, he could in no way commit to writing a brief in support of the proposal.

Indeed, Bob's initial view was that, unless such proposals were implemented within a fuller set of initiatives to expand the economy and increase overall employment, they could well create job losses and significant financial burdens on city governments, as many critics claimed. If so, there was no point in people who are in solidarity with working people and the poor advocating such a policy. Our commitment should never be to any specific policy mechanism, which is merely a means to an end. Our only commitment should be to the end itself. So what if the research led to the conclusion that the living wage proposal was not an effective way of attacking low-wage poverty, or even worse, that it ended up hurting the people it seeks to help? Of course, the job of any self-respecting progressive economist would then be to expose the failings of living wage policies and move on to something better. This was the perspective Bob held as he began researching the project. It was a measure of the high integrity of Madeline Janis-Aparicio and the Los Angeles Living Wage Coalition that they were still willing to support Bob's research after he made his position clear.

The first step Bob took in beginning the project was to talk to experts that he respected in the fields of labor, urban, and regional economics. These included Larry Mishel and John Schmitt of the Economic Policy Institute, Peter Phillips of the University of Utah, Michael Oden of the University of Texas, and David Fairris and Gary Dymski at University of California–Riverside. The proposal for Los Angeles at the time stipulated a living wage minimum of $7.50 an hour and an additional $2.00 in health benefits for workers without private insurance. This would mean a 76 percent wage increase over the then national minimum of $4.25, with health benefits on top of that. The question Bob posed to his colleagues was straightforward: given existing economic conditions, wouldn't such wage standards indeed produce job losses for low-wage workers while also scaring businesses out of Los Angeles, however much we might wish it to be otherwise?

They all gave the same reply, which was "no." Each may have qualified his answer to various degrees, but the basic response was consistent. At the same time, each acknowledged that his intuition regarding living wage proposals reflected his studies of related, but still different questions, including national or statewide minimum wage laws, prevailing wage laws in the construction industry, the relationship between wages and regional employment patterns, and the impact of wage increases on worker productivity. They noted that there had not been any serious examinations specifically of living wage proposals such as that under consideration in Los Angeles.

Bob was nevertheless emboldened to form a team of researchers to conduct a systematic examination of the Los Angeles proposal. This team included Stephanie Luce, who was an advanced graduate student in sociology at the University of Wisconsin–Madison, but happened to be living in Riverside. Stephanie brought areas of expertise to the project that Bob, as well most of the other team members, lacked. In particular, Stephanie was an experienced empirical researcher on labor market issues, having, among other things, worked in research for two years with the U.S. Labor Department in Washington, D.C. The other team members included Bob's UC Riverside faculty colleagues Gary Dymski and Dave Fairris, and UCR graduate students Mark Brenner, Matt Cook, Ted Levine, Marc Schaberg, and Barbara Wiens-Tuers. We also work in close conjunction with Mark Weisbrot and Michelle Sforza-Roderick of the Preamble Center for Public Policy, in Washington, D.C.

After a crash two-month program, our team came up with a result that we could defend on the basis of the evidence we had gathered. We had become convinced that the Los Angeles proposal would bring significant benefits to a small group of the working poor of Los Angeles, without, at the same time, putting serious burdens on either the firms that would fall under the ordinance or on the city itself. In particular, what we found persuasive in our results was that for the overwhelming number of firms that would be affected by the ordinance, the cost increases they would face due to living wage raises would be less than 1 percent of their firms total costs to produce goods and services. This meant that these firms could reasonably be expected to absorb the living wage costs without passing them along to the city. Of course, there would still be a small group of firms for which the cost increases would be far more substantial. But even here, the problem could be readily resolved. We allowed that these firms could pass along most of their new costs, in part to the city through getting more money for their contracts, and in part to consumers through higher prices. But because these firms were relatively small in number, the overall burden on the city and/or consumers would also be small, relative both to the size of the budgets of the city and to the benefits that would accrue to low-wage workers.

We presented these findings to the Los Angeles City Council through several appearances during the fall and winter of 1996–97. Our study generated considerable debate within the media, at the City Council, and in subsequent studies, one sponsored by the Los Angeles Chamber of Commerce, the other, a city-sponsored effort led by a UCLA law professor. We don't know how much influence our work exerted on the direction of the debate, either within or beyond the City Council. The end result, in any case, was that the living wage ordinance passed the City Council unanimously on March 18, 1997, and the City Council subsequently overrode a mayoral veto of the measure on April 1.

Since the passage of the Los Angeles Ordinance, we have been regularly contacted by living wage proponents and municipal government officials throughout the country—including Boston, Cincinnati, Denver, Minneapolis, Oakland, New Haven, Pasadena, and Spokane. We have been eager to share the results of our research and further thoughts. But we also became convinced through these contacts that probably the most useful thing we could do would be to broaden our research beyond our examination of the Los Angeles proposal. We first wanted to explicitly consider a range of other proposals in addition to that in LA. We also wanted to consider the living wage idea in a fuller context. That meant examining experiences with different minimum wage mandates. It also meant understanding the relationship between living wage proposals and various approaches to urban economic development. It finally meant considering the role of national economic policies in creating either a supportive environment or generating obstacles to successful living wage initiatives. By considering this wider set of questions, we were also in a position to honestly examine the limitations of municipal living wage policies as instruments for confronting the problem of low-wage poverty. This book is the result of our explorations to date.

At the same time, we are not so naïve as to assume that this book can serve under all circumstances as a substitute for detailed analyses of how living wage laws would affect a specific community. That is why, in appendix 1, we provide some guidelines as to how researchers at the local level can generate their own results that would be more focused on their own community.

This project has been a large-scale collaboration from its inception, so there are many people who deserve our heartfelt thanks, but not only that. It is equally fitting that that we acknowledge their own contributions on this shared and continuing endeavor.

We must first recognize the inspired work of the Los Angeles Living Wage Coalition and its director, Madeline Janis-Aparicio, not simply in behalf of this book, of course, but to the broader project of bringing economic justice to the United States. We hope our dedication of this book to them makes clear our respect for their work and the work being done by similar organizations throughout the country. Bobbi Murray, the coalition's former publicity director, also made many helpful suggestions as to how to present our arguments in ways that would be comprehensible to people who don't spend their days reading economics textbooks.

This book literally could not have been written without the efforts of the co-authors on the report we prepared on the Los Angeles proposal. The backbone of this book is the database that we constructed together at lightning speed for that earlier project. This book also draws liberally from material drafted by other members of our LA collaboration for that project. We note in the present text where we have incorporated materials initially drafted by our co-workers. So: Gary, Dave, Mark W., Mark B., Marc S., Matt, Ted, Michelle, and Barbara—good work. And equally good work to Karen Smith of the UC–Riverside economics department, who helped Bob get the word out, again and again.

We were assisted in the LA report by numerous officers of the City of Los Angeles. We especially have to single out Mr. Timothy Lynch of the Office of the Controller, council member Jackie Goldberg, and Sharon Delugach of Ms. Goldberg's staff.

Funding for our Los Angeles report came from the Caritas Fund of the Shaler-Adams Foundation, the Liberty Hill Foundation, Wally Marks, and the Roman Catholic Archdiocese of Los Angeles. We appreciate their generosity.

Many people gave us constructive advice and feedback at various stages in this project's evolution. Readers and advisors on our Los Angeles report included Dean Baker, Edie Rasell, Jared Bernstein, John Schmitt, and David Webster at the Economic Policy

Institute; Michel Oden of the University of Texas at Austin; Peter Phillips of the University of Utah; and Keith Griffin of the University of California–Riverside. We also benefited from participants at seminars we presented before the departments of economics at UC–Riverside and at Bob's new academic home, University of Massachusetts–Amherst. Among U-Mass friends, we are especially grateful for the support of Jerry Epstein and Nancy Folbre.

We again drew upon many people in converting this project from a report to its current book form. Dave Fairris and John Schmitt provided careful and constructive comments on chapters 2, 4, and 5, as did Ben Harrison of the New School for Social Research in his reading of chapter 3. Mieke Meurs of American University, Tom Michl of Colgate University, and Eric Nillson of California State University, San Bernadino, were also quite helpful in refereeing our academic paper, from which we draw heavily in chapter 4. That paper is forthcoming in the *Review of Radical Political Economics.*

People who provided useful comments, materials, and suggestions at various stages in the project include Jessica Goodheart and Nari Rhee of the Los Angeles Living Wage Coalition; Amy Hanauer, Center on Wisconsin Strategy; Dennis Houlihan, AFSCME; Jen Kern, ACORN; Linda Lotz, Clergy and Laity United for Economic Justice; Thomas Rick, City of Milwaukee Office of the City Clerk; Bill Robison, City of Portland Office of Finance and Administration; and Bill Spriggs, Joint Economic Committee, U.S. Congress.

Matt Weiland has done an excellent job as The New Press editor of this book. It is not been easy trying to transform a report on one city into a book that tries, all at once, to be broad in its applicability, serious about its economics, and readable. Matt deserves much credit to the extent we have succeeded through his initial enthusiasm for the project, his commitment and patience as we overcame a sputtering start and his skills as an editor.

Finally, we wish to make some individual acknowledgements.

Stephanie: I owe many thanks to Mark Brenner, without whose support I most likely would not have been able to complete this project. Beyond direct contributions to the work, he continued to motivate me to work on and think about the questions posed in this book and elsewhere. I would also like to thank my family—Douglas, Stacey, and Dori—for their general encouragement and patience with my work schedule. I am especially grateful to my late mother, Noreen Luce, who taught me about perseverance and inspired me to work for social justice.

Bob: I would like to thank my parents, Irene and Abe Pollin, for their enthusiastic support and helpful suggestions at many stages of this project. Hannah and Emma Pollin and Sigrid Miller Pollin have done everything short of moving my pen across the page and my cursor across the computer screen. They insisted that I take on this project, they allowed me to occasionally shirk household responsibilities, and they kept reminding me why all the effort was really worth it. I have also gained immeasurably from our daily discussions on the whole myriad of issues that have come up in seeing this project to its present state of completion. I must also single out Emma's detailed reading and incisive comments on the entire book manuscript, which she did amid her own demanding schedule as a college freshman.

Thou shalt not oppress a hired servant that is poor and needy.

—Deuteronomy 24:14

Whenever you hear a speech or read a paper which tells you that the "living wage" is against an "economic law," ask the speaker or writer these questions:

1. What is the actual working of the economic law?

2. In what book on political economy can that law be found? In every case . . . the speaker or writer will be unable to tell you.

—Robert Blanchford, *The Living Wage and the Law of Supply and Demand* (1895)

1 — A Movement for Economic Justice

Anew movement is growing throughout the United States: a movement for living wages. The movement is being built by unions, community groups, and religious organizations. As the movement gathers force, so also has opposition among businesspeople and their political allies. Yet the basic premise of the living wage movement could not be more simple: that anyone in this country who works for a living should not have to raise a family in poverty. Right now, however, nearly eight million families in the United States live in poverty, and more than 60 percent of these families include one or more members who work at jobs. Indeed, more than 20 percent of the country's poor families have at least one family member holding a *full-time* job. These circumstances are likely to only worsen as former recipients of federal welfare support increasingly look for employment to keep themselves and their families afloat. In challenging this situation, the living wage movement has become, in the view of the distinguished journalist Robert Kuttner, "the most interesting (and under-reported) grass roots enterprise to emerge since the civil rights movement."[1]

Minimum wage laws have been in existence for eighty-five years in the U.S., and the national minimum wage was raised most recently to $5.15 in September 1997. But even with this latest increase, the real buying power of the minimum wage after adjusting for inflation was still 30 percent below its peak in 1968—and this despite the fact that the U.S. economy was about 50 percent more productive in 1997 than it was in 1968. More to the point, even at $5.15 an hour, someone who works full-time for 50 weeks would earn only $10,300 a year, which is below the national poverty threshold for a family of two of $10,407. In other words, a single mother with only one child could not keep herself and her child out of poverty through her minimum wage earnings. What about a "traditional" family with one minimum wage worker, one homemaker and two children? With the family's one worker earning $10,300, the family would fall nearly 40 percent below the official poverty threshold of $16,307 for a 4-person family. True, the family would be eligible to receive an earned income tax credit, food stamps, and Medicaid. But the need for such programs to support a family that includes a full-time worker only underscores the fact that the national minimum wage, even after the recent increase, is not close to being a living wage. The living wage movement is thus a movement for family values: the value of adult workers raising children in decent circumstances without having to depend on government subsidies.

Thus far, the living wage movement has emerged primarily at the level of municipal politics. Business opposition within the cities has been stiff. Still, the movement organizers have correctly assessed that their efforts have a greater chance of success when they are targeted at city governments rather than the national or state governments, where the capacity of business to mobilize money and lobbying clout carries greater weight.

The first victory of a municipal living wage movement occurred in Baltimore in 1994. The ordinance there stipulated that firms holding service contracts with the city pay a minimum wage that began at $6.10 an hour in 1996, rising to $7.70 an hour by 1999.

After 1999, Baltimore's living wage minimum would rise in step with the rate of inflation. A single mother working full time at $7.70 an hour would now be able to live with her child above the poverty line. However, the "traditional" family of one worker, one homemaker, and two children would still be living in poverty. The Baltimore "living wage," in other words, is just barely adequate to maintain a family roughly at the poverty line. Nevertheless, in light of the precipitous fall in the national minimum wage over the past thirty years, the Baltimore ordinance represents significant progress.

Within three years of the victory in Baltimore, living wage laws passed in twelve other cities, including New York, Los Angeles, Boston, Milwaukee, Minneapolis and Portland, Oregon. Movements are ongoing in dozens of other cities, including Philadelphia, Denver, and New Orleans. Both the terms and the extent of coverage vary from city to city, but the basic idea of all these ordinances is the same: if private firms want to be eligible for city government contracts, they must pay their workers substantially better than the national minimum wage, since the national minimum wage is a sub-poverty wage. (Appendix 2 documents the range of living wage and related legislation that has been proposed at the municipal, county, or state level in the United States between 1989 and 1997.)

The decline in the national minimum wage to a level well below the poverty line is only one part of a broader set of changes in the United States that has skewed the rewards of economic life increasingly towards the privileged, while rendering life more difficult for most working people as well as the poor. The living wage movement is, correspondingly, a challenge to the basic premises that have guided our economy for a generation.

Perhaps the most dramatic change in overall economic conditions is the decline of average wages, not just for minimum wage workers, but for all workers below the supervisory level. As figure 1.1 shows, the average hourly wage for nonsupervisory workers peaked in 1973 at $14.23 (in 1997 dollars). Moving into the late 1970s, the average wage declines fairly steadily through 1993 and begins to rise only slightly thereafter. As of 1997, the average wage for nonsupervisory workers was $12.24, 14 percent below the 1973 peak, even though the economy was experiencing its seventh straight year of expansion and by this point productivity was 34 percent greater than in 1973.

The decline in average wages also reflects an increasing concentration of wealth and income that has accompanied it. Thus, for example, in 1968, the income of the richest 5 percent of households was 16 times greater than the poorest 20 percent, reflecting an already formidable level of economic inequality. However, as of 1994, the income of the richest 5 percent of households had grown to a level 24 times greater than the poorest 20 percent.

The trends of declining wages and increasing income and wealth concentration correspond to several other changes in national policy. The first has been the growing hostility of business toward unions and the corresponding decline in union membership. Union representation reached its postwar peak in 1954 at the time of the merger of the AFL-CIO, when roughly 35 percent of all nonfarm workers belonged to unions. This number began falling sharply in the 1970s, when corporations began a deliberate offensive, what former UAW President Douglas Fraser termed a "one-sided class war" against unions. This continuing class war has pushed wages downward, since, on average, workers at the same skill level per-

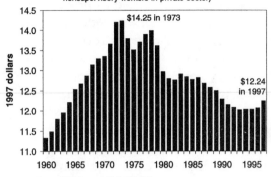

Figure 1.1
Real Wages in the United States, 1960-1997
(average hourly earnings for production or
nonsupervisory workers in private sector)

Source: U.S. Bureau of Labor Statistics.
Note: Figures for 1997 are through 11/97.

forming similar jobs make about 20 percent more if they work in union shops. Another measure of the declining power of workers at their jobs has been the rise of contingent workers—those who hold jobs with virtually no job security, and thus almost no power to resist efforts by businesses to push wages downward. Conservatively estimated, contingent workers now constitute about 10 percent of the total workforce.

Urban economic policy has also become increasingly an instrument of the wealthy and dismissive of the needs of the nonwealthy. Since at least the early 1980s, city governments have pursued "urban development" policies that actively seek to attract businesses to locate within their cities by offering them a wide array of subsidies and other enticements. Huge financial resources have been devoted to these efforts. In 1993, for example, Mercedes Benz located just outside Birmingham, Alabama, after receiving a subsidy package amounting to a projected $168,000 per job, with no penalty for Mercedes if it fails to create the number of jobs it has promised to provide. Such policies have not, on the whole, succeeded in creating new jobs, reducing urban poverty, or reversing the decline of urban communities, even when, as is the case in some areas, they have promoted the growth of downtown businesses. Indeed, despite rapid economic growth and low unemployment in 1997, the U.S. Conference of Mayors found that requests for emergency food had risen by 16 percent relative to 1996, the largest increase in five years. The mayors cited low wages as a major cause of the surging demand for emergency food.

National economic policy has also been skewed toward the rich. The political agenda of Wall Street dominates Federal Reserve policy, and the Federal Reserve in turn is the predominant force in formulating and implementing national economic policy. But what is Wall Street's agenda? Its concerns are often expressed as an adamant opposition to inflationary pressures that may result through reducing unemployment. Wall Street is indeed opposed to even modest inflation—even when it is associated with increasing economic growth—because inflation means that the value of existing assets traded on financial markets might decline. But even this is not the primary concern of Wall Street. Its more fundamental commitment is to prevent workers from getting enough bargaining power to force up wages and grab a larger share of national income. This commitment is often expressed in terms of a fear of low unemployment. But what we have seen most recently is that low unemployment is acceptable as long as wages don't rise. This enables the distribution of income and wealth to become increasingly concentrated.

But national economic policy has been even more explicit in its harsh treatment of working people and the poor. In the summer of 1996, President Clinton ended "welfare as we know it" by signing a bill requiring all welfare recipients to take jobs of some sort and by devolving control over most aspects of welfare to state governments. In fact, the new welfare law only accelerated a trend that had actually been underway for years, as more and more states obtained exemptions from federal regulations to permit local "experiments." There is no doubt that welfare policy was in disarray prior to the new Clinton program. However, it is also clear that the Clinton policies will push wages downward within the low-wage labor market, as more people enter this market competing for jobs. Prof. Chris Tilly of the University of Massachusetts estimated, for example, that in New York City, wages at the low end of the job market could fall by as much as 9 or 10 percent due to the welfare overhaul. By the end of 1997, *Business Week* reported "increasing evidence that millions of single mothers . . . are being driven further into poverty." The problem, they write, is not a lack of jobs, but rather that "the work many mothers find pays so little that their incomes are lower than they were on welfare."[2]

The living wage movement is resisting these dominant trends and posing an alternative economic vision, making it an effective voice for economic justice in the United States. The living wage movement, in other words, is not simply concerned with improving wages for workers employed by businesses holding municipal government contracts, even though this is the immediate target of their efforts. The living wage movement is committed to reversing the economy-wide wage squeeze, stopping tax giveaways to big business, reenergizing the labor movement, and ending the war on the poor. This broader set of commitments was expressed clearly by Madeline Janis-Aparicio, director of the Los Angeles Living Wage Coalition, which was organized by several unions in the LA area. In her view, the goals of the Los Angeles living wage campaign were to "directly affect the lives of workers who are getting a raise; to develop a tool for union organizing and to promote successful organizing actions; and to raise the public issue of the need for a living wage, the problem of wage inequity, and a certain level of dignified treatment for workers."

The New Party and ACORN (the Association of Community Organizations for Reform Now) are the two national organizations outside of the union movement that have been particularly active in promoting the living wage movement. From their perspective as well, the goals of the movement are broad-gauged. Thus, Tammy Johnson, an organizer with Progressive Milwaukee, an affiliate of the New Party, believes that the living wage campaigns have had significant impact beyond the passage of the ordinances themselves. She says "I think the phrase 'living wage job' is in the vocabulary now in a way that it wasn't two or three years ago. When jobs are being created, people will ask, 'is it a livable wage job?'"

Johnson thinks running living wage campaigns all over Wisconsin has helped "build support for a statewide minimum wage increase. People we meet support it. Most people see lay-offs and downsizing, and believe companies have no loyalty to their workers. They want minimum wage increases because it will trickle into their community. And they support it from the idea of fairness. It rings true to people." Similarly, Johnson says that local living wage campaigns "helped to get the federal minimum wage increase passed. Legislators saw that people around the country supported the idea, and realized that they should pass it or they might not get re-elected."[3]

Support from religious organizations has also been tied to a broader agenda for equality and economic fairness. Indeed, the first living wage movement in Baltimore was begun after a church group, Baltimoreans United In Leadership Development, noticed an increase in people with jobs using its soup kitchens. The group then joined with the American Federation of State, County, and Municipal Employees (AFSCME) to form the local living wage movement. In Los Angeles, a prominent rabbi and the bishops of both the Episcopal and Methodist churches co-authored a *Los Angeles Times* opinion article which made such a broader commitment clear, stating emphatically that "we have a right and responsibility to see that . . . employees are paid enough to support themselves and their families in basic dignity."[4] Moreover, after the passage of the living wage ordinance, the Southern California Ecumenical Council passed a resolution calling on all religious institutions to themselves pay all their own workers a living wage.

Polling data show broad general support for a living wage minimum. A *Los Angeles Times* poll conducted just prior to the vote of the LA City Council on its living wage proposal found that 70 percent of the respondents favored the initiative. A range of surveys taken prior to the increase in the national minimum wage in 1996 generated similar levels of support for the raise, i.e., between 70 and 80 percent of respondents favored the increase.

The living wage movement has thus received strong, passionate leadership from community, union, and religious groups and widespread support among the general public. But the business opposition has been similarly forceful, often in cooperation with major city officials. Norm Coleman, the Democratic mayor of St. Paul, Minnesota, termed the proposal there a "knee-jerk, liberal, quick-fix attempt at social engineering that would have a disastrous impact upon jobs and economic growth in St. Paul." In Los Angeles, the deputy mayor for economic development Gary Mendoza went even further, claiming the ordinance could mean that "entire industries could be wiped out or move overseas." In Houston, the opposition Save Jobs for Houston Committee put out numerous ads and mailings with the message that the ordinance would lead to "Cops and firefighters yanked off the streets. Higher taxes. Thousands of jobs lost. Soaring prices for such essentials as food and prescription drugs. The wholesale destruction of small businesses. Streets riddled with potholes. Swollen welfare rolls."

Some business groups have been more sober in their assessments, but still strongly in opposition. For example, Mary Jo Paque from the Metropolitan Milwaukee Association of Commerce argues that "business feels that the ordinance sends a double message to business, in particular with regard to subsidies. It says 'come to Wisconsin and we will invest in your success,' but then it is placing obstacles in their way, and not really helping them." In Duluth, Minnesota, the chairman of the board of the Duluth Chamber of Commerce says, "I'm less concerned about what the ordinance says than I am with the signal we're sending here. Realistically, there isn't anything in this ordinance that's scary, but for those who don't read the fine print, the fact that we have such an ordinance will just be another check mark against us, one that other communities don't have to deal with."[5]

Rhetoric aside, the arguments of the opponents of the living wage proposals cannot be dismissed. The cruelest pitfalls in economic policy-making result from the "law of unintended consequences," doing harm while seeking to do good. Those who are naturally sympathetic to living wage proposals have a special responsibility to examine whether such policies would in fact deliver the benefits claimed. Indeed, we have been preoccupied from the beginning of our research with the law of unintended consequences. Like Hippocrates, we have been committed to the principle of 'first, do no harm,' and we have therefore been especially wary of advocating a proposal that appears to make sense but actually does not. It is in this spirit that advocates of living wages need to take a good hard look at both their own presuppositions as well as the claims of critics.

Many of the arguments against living wage proposals parallel those made against national and statewide minimum wage laws, and indeed, against the very principle of a legislated wage minimum. The most common criticism focuses on employment effects. That is, even if the living standard of directly affected workers were to rise because of an increased minimum wage, wouldn't the new wage floor also reduce job opportunities by pricing unskilled workers out of the market in which they are competing for jobs? This effect would particularly harm the unemployed as well as employed low-wage workers, i.e., the very people that the laws are purportedly seeking to help.

Critics have also argued that a minimum wage increase would weaken firms who hire a high proportion of low-wage workers. Some of these firms could fail through having to pay excessive minimum wages, thus again reducing employment for low-wage workers. But to the extent that some firms can handle such mandated cost increases, it would be primarily because these firms are able to pass on their higher labor costs through raising prices. Consumers would now be the victims because the law had required that low-wage workers be paid more than the market deems they are worth.

Additional arguments have also been made specifically against the municipal living wage proposals, and these positions are reflected in some of the opposition's rhetoric. It is, of course, true that a living wage mandate would increase the regulatory burden on businesses affected by the law. Wouldn't this burden create incentives for firms to relocate to areas that do not have a living wage requirement? Critics argue that losing businesses in this way to other localities can only worsen a city's problems of unemployment and poverty. But even if businesses did remain within the municipality, they would, as much as possible, pass their additional costs onto the city governments themselves. This would place new strains on cities' already overstretched budgets, perhaps forcing painful cuts in other city efforts to benefit low-income families.

The main purpose of this book is to assess the merits of these arguments against the claims of living wage supporters that such measures would significantly benefit the working poor. In chapter 2 we ask the standard questions on minimum wage mandates. Do low-wage workers suffer from increased unemployment when minimum wages rise? Do the benefits of minimum wage laws flow disproportionately to middle-class teenagers? Do municipal minimum wage laws disturb the local business climate and add burdensome costs to city governments? All of these claims turn out to be false. The evidence shows that low-income working people, the targeted beneficiaries of minimum wage laws, do in fact receive most of the wage gains. Unemployment rates, moreover, do not correlate with changes in the minimum wage. Indeed, to the extent there is any statistical relationship, it is that unemployment *declines* when the national minimum wage rises. This does not suggest that a rising minimum wage *causes* unemployment to decline, but rather that other factors in the economy are more significant in determining unemployment rates. The most important of these is the overall demand for goods and services, which in turn will increase demand for low-wage workers.

Turning specifically to the early experience with Baltimore's municipal living wage ordinance, we find no evidence that this has produced any significant changes in Baltimore's overall economic performance. For example, the total dollar amount for city contracts that were renewed in the first year after Baltimore implemented its living wage ordinance actually *fell* slightly relative to their pre–living wage levels.

The conclusion of chapter 2 is therefore that the various types of minimum wage laws have been viable policy tools for raising living standards of the working poor, and that the negative effects anticipated by opponents do not emerge from the data. This does not mean that there are no limits on how high minimum wages can be set before some negative effects would result. But we are apparently far from approaching such limits, given that the wage declines experienced by most working people over the past generation have occurred while the economy's productive capacity has grown.

In chapter 3 we examine living wage proposals in the context of urban economic policies more generally. For the most part, as we have noted earlier, urban economic policies at least since the early 1980s have meant providing various vehicles through which city governments could channel subsides to private businesses. We consider the effect of these policies along three lines—their impact on economic growth, on job creation, and on inequality. There is no doubt, to begin with, that businesses will be attracted to localities if subsidies are large enough. But the key question here is, at what point does a subsidy become "large enough"? If neighboring municipalities all offer equivalent subsidies, then the advantage to any one municipality is lost, no matter what the dollar amount offered. In such situations, all municipalities will have simply foregone government revenue, but none would be relatively more alluring to businesses. In fact, the evidence shows that the benefits to any one municipality of a business subsidy strategy have dissipated as ever-increasing numbers of them came to adopt the same approach.

But we then consider another crucial point. Even allowing that one municipality might attract new firms through a business subsidy strategy, are these newly created jobs, or are they simply jobs that one area has poached from other areas? Unless, on a national basis, the subsidy strategy is concentrated in areas of high unemployment, municipal governments end up financing mere poaching operations. The evidence we review in chapter 3 shows that poaching has dominated net job creation.

Chapter 3 then considers another strategy that municipal governments have adopted increasingly since the late 1980s, the practice of contracting out government services to private firms, or "outsourcing." The primary reason cities outsource is that private contractors pay lower wages and offer far less generous benefits to workers. Outsourcing therefore saves money for cities through producing lower living standards for workers. But does it improve their delivery of services to residents? In fact, despite the widely touted claim that private sector firms are inherently more efficient than the government, outsourcing invites inefficiency and corruption in the delivery of government services. This is because outsourcing encourages firms to compete through influence-peddling, public relations and, not infrequently, straight-out bribes.

At the same time, for municipal governments even to bargain effectively with potential contractors, they must retain both the expertise to be knowledgeable purchasers and the capacity to, at times, refuse all bids and provide services themselves. Phoenix, Arizona, has been successful at pursuing such an approach—a "public/private competitive process"—since the late 1970s. But for this strategy to be viable, the public sector cannot be placed at a disadvantage through allowing private firms to make "lowball" bids because they pay their workers sub-poverty wages. Here the need to impose a living wage minimum on private firms could not be more clear.

But are there viable alternative municipal policies—that is, policies that are compatible with a living wage minimum and may even be supportive of high wages as a component of an urban development program? We attempt only a brief sketch in chapter 3. The fact is that businesses can benefit in many ways through locating within cities: their suppliers and markets are close by; large skilled labor pools are also more accessible; and the efficiency gains from infrastructure spending can be spread more effectively among a larger number of firms. Cities need to build on these natural advantages. In doing so, establishing a living wage minimum makes clear the types of firms cities will want to attract, retain, or promote. What is evident since the ascendancy of the business-subsidy strategy is that not all businesses will make positive contributions to the social development of cities. In particular, firms that are unwilling to pay living wages provide a dubious foundation on which to attack the problems of urban poverty and inequality.

In chapter 4, we concentrate our attention on the municipal living wage proposals themselves. We consider three separate proposals.

The first is based on that which became law in the City of Milwaukee in 1995. This ordinance applies only to certain types of firms holding service contracts with the city—legal, engineering, and architectural firms, for example, are exempt. For the affected service contractors, the ordinance mandates a minimum hourly wage just sufficient to enable one worker to support a family of three at the national poverty line. The actual wage rate is therefore indexed to adjustments in the national poverty threshold. As we write, that hourly wage rate is $6.43.

The second version of a living wage ordinance is based on that which became law in Los Angeles in March 1997. It has substantially broader coverage than the Milwaukee law. A higher proportion of service contractors are covered in the Los Angeles law, but also, more significantly, firms receiving large city subsidies as well as firms holding concession agreements with the city, such as airport concessionaires, are also covered. The city concessionaires, in particular, will tend to employ relatively large concentrations of low-wage workers. The Los Angeles ordinance sets the minimum wage at $7.25. It also includes health benefits of up to $1.25 per hour for workers without private health insurance, and requires up to twelve paid days off per year for all workers.

Finally, we examine the type of proposal put forward as propositions but defeated in both Denver in the November 1996 election and Houston in January 1997. These were straightforward, citywide minimum wage ordinances, applying to all workers within the city limits. The minimum hourly wage in both cases was set at $6.50. These proposals did not have any provisions for health benefits or paid days off.

We consider all of these proposals in the context of the Los Angeles economy, and refer to them as Plan X (the Milwaukee-type proposal as applied to Los Angeles), Plan Y (the LA proposal itself) and Plan Z (the 1996 Denver-Houston proposal in the Los Angeles context). This enables us to make direct comparisons of the extent of coverage among these three approaches. Clearly, the Milwaukee-type Plan X would have the most narrow impact. We find that about 470 firms and 1,400 workers would fall under the terms of the ordinance. With Plan Y, as we discuss in Chapter 4, the extent of coverage is ambiguous. Our broadest projection shows that nearly 1,000 firms and 7,600 workers are affected—i.e., double the number of firms and five times the number of workers as in Plan X. Of course, Plan Z, establishing universal coverage for the living wage within the municipality, has far greater reach than either Plans X or Y. Here both the numbers of firms and workers affected by the proposal would range in the hundreds of thousands.

We produce estimates of the total cost increases of these three proposals, and then in each case measure these costs relative to the total costs of producing goods and services by the firms affected by the ordinances. This is where we find that the wage and benefit increases for most firms due to the living wage requirements would be *less than 1 percent of these firms' total costs to produce goods and services*. As such, the living wage ordinances are likely to have negligible effects on these businesses, which we term "low-impact firms." The living wage is also likely to have negligible effects on the budgets of municipal governments, as long as the governments do not concede that the cost increases generated by the ordinances should, as a matter of course, be absorbed by themselves. In practice, city governments may choose to cave in to the inevitable demands by businesses for better contract terms after the businesses are forced to pay living wages. Our point is that they need not do so.

We did of course find that a small number of firms that employ a high concentration of low-wage workers—"high-impact" firms such as food concessionaires at airports—will face increases between 10 and 30 percent of total costs in meeting the living wage requirements. But even here, the municipal budgetary impact of cost pass-throughs by high-impact firms can be limited after allowing that: (1) many of the high-impact firms, like airport concessionares, also have the option of modestly raising prices; (2) the ordinances will necessarily be phased in gradually, as existing contracts run out and new ones are bid on; and (3) if need be, *the rate of improvement* in city services can be reduced slightly as the living wage is phased in.

Perhaps the largest single cost to municipalities would be tax losses in a city- or county-wide ordinance, such as Plan Z, due to business relocations out of the boundaries of the municipality. But even here the likely revenue losses are small relative to the wage gains to workers and the total revenue base of municipalities. Moreover, the more limited Plans X and Y, affecting only firms that have contracts with the municipalities, should not induce any business relocations. This is because firms holding city contracts would fall under the terms of the ordinance regardless of whether they were located within or outside the city—whether, for example, they were in Milwaukee working on a Milwaukee city contract or in Chicago, holding that same contract.

In short, the evidence we present in chapter 4 is the foundation on which we reach our most basic conclusion, that there is no reason why a municipal living wage ordinance should be seen as seriously burdensome for cities. Moreover, to reach this conclusion, our analysis does not rely at all on making implausible assumptions about how a city's economic performance will dramatically improve after a living wage ordinance takes effect. Quite the contrary, our analysis assumes no significant departures from the normal operations of municipal economies.

Our chapter 4 analysis does, however, include one important assumption, which could be producing *overestimates* of the effects of living wage ordinances. We assume that firms falling under the terms of the ordinances actually abide by the law, compensating their employees as the law stipulates. From the experience in several cities, we know that this will not happen automatically. In Los Angeles, for example, the mayor's office strongly opposed the ordinance that passed in March 1997, and has subsequently sought to provide exemptions from the law for as many businesses as possible. Correspondingly, the city's professional staff responsible for enforcement has been less than vigilant in its initial efforts. This and similar experiences elsewhere make clear that living wage supporters cannot assume their job is done once a law has been passed. They are the only ones, in the end, who can make the law stick—through informing affected workers and businesses of their rights and obligations and insisting that government officials fulfill their responsibilities. One factor that will facilitate the job of enforcement by living wage supporters is that firms abiding by the law have an incentive to monitor their competitors, especially in cases where complying firms lose government contracts to violators.

In chapter 5, we examine who benefits from living wage ordinances. The most obvious beneficiaries are the low-wage workers who receive raises and their families. We consider two cases, the Plan Y scenario of a raise to $7.25, plus $1.25 in health benefits and 12 paid days off; and Plan Z, in which workers are raised to a $6.50 minimum but receive no additional benefits.

In both cases, we find that the average worker will receive a raise in pretax income of more than 30 percent. However, what this means in terms after-tax spending power and benefits will depend on the size of the worker's family, since tax rates and eligibility for the earned income tax credit, food stamps, and subsidized medical care will vary with family size. We estimate the case for our "traditional family" of one worker, one homemaker, and two children. After accounting for taxes and all forms of government support available to this family, the living wage will still bring a hefty increase in their disposable income—on the order of between 7 and 13 percent.

This family will also receive substantial, if less direct, additional benefits. The first is that the family will now have significantly greater access to bank loans and other forms of credit that can be used to purchase a home or automobile or to finance higher education. The second is that as workers move into a higher tax bracket, they become less dependent on government subsidies to sustain themselves. Workers' sense of self-worth should therefore rise as they become more self-reliant. This is the same point—indeed perhaps the only point—on which everyone could agree in considering welfare reform: that earning a dollar of income is far superior to being given a dollar of government subsidies, in terms of a person's self-image and attitude toward life and work.

Workers and their families are not the only beneficiaries of the living wage ordinance. As the low-wage family comes to rely far less on government support to keep themselves afloat, the corollary is that the government spends correspondingly less to help working people survive the effects of earning sub-poverty wages. The other main beneficiaries of living wage policies may come as something of a surprise. We argue that the firms employing a high concentration of low-wage workers will themselves benefit through establishing a living wage standard. This is because the raises to the low-wage workers will reduce absenteeism and turnover, i.e., the rate at which workers quit their jobs and firms then have to replace them. Burdened with having to find replacement workers four times a year for each of the jobs at his plant, Henry Ford was perhaps the first U.S. businessperson to recognize that higher wages would stabilize his work force. He decided to nearly double wages at Ford Motors in 1913 to $5.00 a day, and almost completely eliminated turnover with this single stroke.

Focusing on our contemporary period, we present interviews with managers of firms in Los Angeles who had been paying living wages voluntarily before the living wage ordinance itself became law. These managers state unequivocally that their firms run more efficiently because they pay living wages. Operating more efficiently in turn enables these firms to compete with businesses that insist on paying minimum wages. One of the benefits of living wage ordinances is that they should force many firms now paying sub-poverty wages to transform themselves—i.e., to raise efficiency through creating a high-wage, high-morale work environment.

In short, municipal living wage policies are effective at delivering higher living standards for low-wage workers and their families; reducing government subsidy payments to these working families; and lowering turnover and absenteeism for firms with high concentrations of low-wage workers. At the same time, as we saw in chapter 4, the costs of living wage programs can be readily diffused among firms, consumers, and municipal governments such that these costs need not be burdensome for any affected group.

This conclusion certainly helps make the case for municipal living wage policies. At the same time, for those concerned with the broader aim of eradicating low-wage poverty and not just demonstrating the viability of any specific living wage program—and here we would include virtually all of the many thousands of living wage movement supporters—these results are not entirely favorable. This is because most of what makes either Plan X (based on the Milwaukee proposal) or Plan Y (the LA ordinance) affordable is that, relatively speaking, their impact is small. Even our most extensive Plan Y projections show that roughly 7,600 full- and part-time workers would receive direct wage increases. This amounts to no more than 0.3 percent of the total workforce in Los Angeles County of 2.3 million workers. As we discuss in chapter 4, perhaps another 10,000 will receive health benefits, paid days off, and "ripple effect" wage gains. The "ripple effect" increases would go to workers already earning above the living wage. Their raises, which would not be mandated, would follow from the mandated living wage raises as firms adjust their pay scales up their job ladders. But even after we allow for this factor, the overall effect of municipal living wage policies will still be tiny in the context of the entire Los Angeles workforce, and would be similarly small in other cities.

Such a result invites us to consider the prospects for a greatly broadened, preferably a national living wage policy. This is the issue we address in our closing chapter 6. Something akin to this idea was already advanced in Congress in 1997 by Sen. Edward Kennedy and Rep. David Bonior. But their plan was still modest—a rise in the hourly minimum wage to $7.25 by 2002. After allowing for inflation through 2002, the Kennedy-Bonior proposal would still leave minimum wage workers and their families mired in poverty.

Something much closer to an authentic national living wage policy did exist in the late 1960s, when the national minimum wage was approximately equal to the four-person poverty threshold. The question we therefore pursue in chapter 6 is, what would be needed to recreate the wage standards that prevailed in the 1960s? Or to pose the same issue from another angle, what has changed so drastically over the past thirty years that—despite the economy's far greater productive capacity—the idea of a national living wage now strikes many as pie-in-the-sky?

We argue in chapter 6 that the thirty-year plummeting of the minimum wage should be understood as as part of the larger transition of the post–World War II U.S. economy from a "golden" to a "leaden" age. The golden age, lasting roughly from the end of World War II through the 1960s, was characterized by rapid economic growth, low unemployment, mild business cycles, and rising living standards, especially for the white male sector of the working class. By contrast, the leaden age has been distinguished by slow growth, high unemployment, more severe business cycles, and stagnating or declining living standards for the majority.

We have already mentioned some of the main fac-

tors contributing to the transition from the golden to
the leaden age. These include the attack on unions
and the rise of the contingent labor market. Another
major factor has been globalization. Of course, the
term "globalization" has by now reached the status of
a ubiquitous, if vaguely understood, buzzword. For
our purposes, it refers to the rise of trade competition
and the increasing mobility of U.S. multinational
firms. It has meant that U.S. workers are placed in an
increasingly competitive posture against workers in
countries with wage scales far below those in the United
States. But perhaps even more forcefully, globalization
has meant that U.S. firms can threaten to leave a community if workers try to push up wages. The result has
been sustained downward wage pressure.

Another factor contributing to the leaden age has
been what we might term the "financialization" of the
economy. Here we are referring to the explosion of
financial market trading as well as the increased integration of the U.S. financial market with those of the
rest of the world. Among other effects, financialization has forced a shift in the goals of national economic policy. As noted earlier, the Federal Reserve has
become the only real player in national policy-making
and basically acts in behalf of the perceived best interests of Wall Street. This means that the overriding
commitment of the Fed is to protect the values of
financial assets rather than expand the production of
new goods and services, which would in turn create
more jobs and encourage upward wage pressure.

Recognizing these leaden age economic forces, we
argue in chapter 6 that the key to creating a national
living wage would be to pursue policies which do two
things: increase the economy's growth rate to a level
closer to that of the golden age; and create an environment in which the benefits of growth are shared in

a more equitable fashion. The chapter then discusses some of the types of policies that can achieve this, even after taking the full measure of the barriers to success created by globalization, financialization, and aggressive anti-union business practices.

Such policies move us well beyond the framework of municipal wage policies themselves. But we are not minimizing the significance of municipal living wage movements towards defining an agenda for economic justice in the United States. The great merit of the living wage movement is that, as it expands from city to city, it becomes more deeply interwoven into the country's political and economic fabric. But getting into the national consciousness is not enough. The real point is to win the argument.

2—Minimum Wage, Prevailing Wage, Living Wage

The living wage ordinances that have passed or are being considered throughout the country are one type of minimum wage law. Several other such laws have been in existence in the United States at various levels of government since 1912. In assessing the viability of living wage proposals, it will be useful to consider here the experiences with this range of existing minimum wage laws.

The most familiar type of minimum wage law is one with near-universal coverage, that is, one applying to virtually all workers in the country, state, or municipality, depending on the government body establishing the law.[1] Such laws are obviously much broader in coverage than most of the living wage ordinances that have been proposed, which apply only to workers employed by firms holding government contracts.

The first statewide minimum wage law was passed in Massachusetts in 1912. Over the next decade, sixteen states and the District of Columbia followed with similar laws. The constitutionality of minimum wage legislation was challenged almost immediately, and in 1923, the U.S. Supreme Court declared the District of Columbia's law unconstitutional. However, the Court reconsidered the issue several times subsequently, and reversed itself in 1937, setting the stage for the national minimum-wage regulations enacted as part of the Fair Labor Standards Act of 1938. This law, as amended, forms the basis for federal minimum wage legislation today. The initial minimum set by the Fair Labor Standards Act was 25 cents an hour.

The primary argument the early supporters gave for establishing minimum wage laws, identical to that of living wage proponents today, was simple: people working at full-time jobs should be able to provide a decent life for themselves and their families. Indeed, as Lawrence Glickman documents in his illuminating study, *A Living Wage: American Workers and the Making of Consumer Society*, the movement for minimum wage legislation itself grew out of the *living wage* movement that began in the United States after the 1877 national railroad strike. The early U.S. living wage movement had, in turn, followed similar developments that began in British labor struggles in the early 1870s.

Glickman explains that considerable ambiguity existed from the beginning in defining what exactly constituted a "living wage." But the guiding principle was clear: "Although proponents differed over the cash value of a living wage, the phrase became in the [post–Civil War] years what the term "full fruits of labor" was to the antebellum era, namely, shorthand for economic justice."[2]

Religious groups were strong supporters of the living wage movement from its inception. One of the early works written in behalf of minimum wage legislation was a 1906 book by Monsignor John A. Ryan titled *A Living Wage: Its Ethical and Economic Aspects*. More broadly, as Sar Levitan and Richard Belous write in *More Than Subsistence*, "A 'social gospel' was taken up by several religious leaders who saw the abuses of industrialization as a sharp contradiction with moral teachings, and the first American minimum wage campaigns took on elements of a religious revival."[3]

With the coming of the Depression and New Deal in the 1930s, supporters advanced another argument for the minimum wage: that it would help boost workers' buying power and thus stimulate overall demand for goods and services in the economy. This point was explicitly recognized, for example, in the debate over the Fair Labor Standards Act. Since the 1930s, variations on the same two points—that the minimum wage provides a modicum of fairness to low-wage workers and that it benefits the economy generally by boosting overall demand—have been the central arguments in behalf of national minimum wage laws.

The national Davis-Bacon law and the "little Davis-Bacons" at the state level are the best-known minimum wage laws with more narrow coverage. These established "prevailing wage" standards for construction firms working under government contracts. The 1931 federal prevailing wage law was sponsored by Republican senator James J. Davis from Pennsylvania, a former secretary of labor, and Rep. Robert L. Bacon, a Republican banker from New York, and was signed into law that year by Herbert Hoover. Seven states preceded the federal government in creating a prevailing wage minimum for government construction projects. The first state law was passed in 1891 in Kansas. Overall, forty-two states at one time had prevailing wage standards—"little Davis-Bacon" laws—in place.

The main motivation for the Davis-Bacon laws, as with the minimum wage laws, was to ensure that workers could earn a livelihood from a full-time job. But supporters of these laws were also concerned about the quality of work performed by contractors who bid low on government projects. They wanted to discourage such aggressively low bids, since firms would often hire unqualified workers to do the work.

But what is a "prevailing" wage? In 1935, Secretary of Labor Frances Perkins defined the prevailing wage as that paid to the majority of workers in an area. If there was no single wage that a majority of workers earned, then the "modal" wage—the wage most frequently earned by the workers in the area—would prevail as long as at least 30 percent of workers earned that wage. The prevailing wage was set as the average wage in the area if no given wage rate was paid to at least 30 percent of all workers. In practice, the "prevailing" wage has generally been the rate paid to union workers in an area. This has led both to a relatively high wage scale in government construction jobs and to a legitimization of the role of unions in the building trades.

There are two other federal laws whose terms are similar to those of Davis-Bacon. The Walsh-Healey Act, implemented in 1936, requires firms that hold supply contracts with the federal government to pay their employees prevailing wages. The McNamara-O'Hara Act, or the Federal Service Contract Act, which became law in 1965, requires that certain classes of workers (primarily blue-collar) on federal service contracts be paid the prevailing wage of that locality.[4] In 1976, the act was expanded to cover all categories of workers on federal service contracts except executive, administrative, and professional workers. The government's motivation in agreeing to pay the private sector's prevailing wage to its suppliers and service contractors through these laws was to prevent the government orders of supplies and services from affecting private sector wage scales.

While the Davis-Bacon Act and its statewide equivalents have had substantial impact, the other two prevailing wage mandates have been less significant. In the case of the Walsh-Healey Act, a 1963 court ruling declared that all wage determinations under the act were subject to court challenge and the Department of Labor has not pursued enforcement of the act since that time. The Service Contract Act is still enforced, although several industry and employer groups have succeeded in winning exemptions. While there are no official records as to how many workers it covers, the AFL-CIO estimates coverage at 600,000 workers as of 1995.

THE MINIMUM WAGE AND POVERTY

Most evidence suggests that minimum wage laws with near-universal coverage are successful at providing better wages to the working poor. For example, in examining who received raises from the 1996–97 two-stage increase in the minimum wage from $4.25 to $5.15, Jared Bernstein of the Economic Policy Institute found the following:

1. Close to 10 million workers—8.9 percent all people with jobs—benefit from the full increase to $5.15;
2. These workers are mostly female (58 percent) and adult (71 percent);
3. Nearly half of the affected workers (46 percent) work full time, while another 33 percent work between 20 and 34 hours per week;
4. The increase primarily benefits low-income families—57 percent of the gains from the increase go to the poorest 40 percent of working families.[5]

The minimum wage, in short, has proven effective at getting benefits to their intended recipients. Despite this, the minimum wage has had only limited, and diminishing, impact in addressing the problem of low-wage poverty. The reason is simple: the real buying power of the minimum wage (after adjusting for inflation) has fallen substantially over the past 30 years. Even after the October 1997 increase to $5.15, the minimum wage still provides a full-time worker with 19 percent less income than that needed just to maintain a family of three at the poverty line and 37 percent less income than necessary to support a family of four at the poverty line.[6] We can see this more clearly through considering figure 2.1.

Figure 2.1
Real Value of United States Minimum
Wage, 1960-1997
(in 1997 dollars)

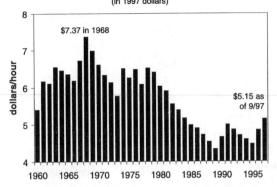

One Full-Time Minimum Wage Income as a Percentage
of three-person Family Poverty Threshold

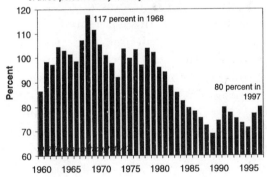

1997 figures are through 11/97.

The upper panel of figure 2.1 shows the real value for the minimum wage, expressed in constant 1997 dollars. We see that the minimum wage rose through the early 1960s and peaked in 1968 at $7.37. Since then, the minimum wage has been falling. It declined most sharply through the 1980s. Even after the September 1997 increase to $5.15, the inflation-adjusted value of the minimum wage was still 30 percent below the 1968 peak.

This steep decline in the real value of the minimum wage has meant that the minimum wage has been less and less effective as a tool for preventing poverty even among low-wage workers with full-time jobs. We see this in the lower panel of figure 2.1, which plots values for the minimum wage as a percentage of the official poverty threshold for a three-person family. As the table shows, in 1960, a full-time worker earning the minimum wage would earn about 86 percent of the poverty-threshold income for a family of three. The ratio then peaks in 1968 at 117 percent. After the September 1997 increase to a $5.15 minimum, a full-time worker at that pay rate would still earn only 80 percent of the poverty-threshold living standard for a family of three.

THE MINIMUM WAGE AND EMPLOYMENT

Despite the inadequacy of the national minimum wage rate as an anti-poverty tool, the most severe critics of minimum wages actually contend that its effects are too strong, not too weak. The critics believe that *any* government-mandated minimum higher than the market-established wage will reduce employment opportunities for workers. In particular, those most likely to suffer employment losses through the minimum wage laws will be the less-skilled, low-wage job seekers. As such, minimum wage laws only serve to harm the very people they are intended to help.

It is important to distinguish here between _employment_ loss and changes in the _unemployment rate_. Employment losses due to the minimum wage would mean that workers are laid off because their employers are unwilling to pay them the mandated minimum and they are not hired elsewhere. This will also bring an increase in the _unemployment rate_, which measures the proportion of workers actively seeking jobs who are unable to obtain them. However, the unemployment rate can also rise because low-income people who are out of the labor market might begin seeking jobs after the minimum wage has risen. Increases in the unemployment rate that occur for this reason should not, however, be regarded as a negative consequence of the minimum wage.

Keeping this in mind, it is nevertheless useful to examine the relationship between the minimum wage and the _unemployment rate_, since the unemployment rate is the standard, if rough, indicator of overall labor market conditions.

Does the minimum wage lead to employment losses and/or higher unemployment? We consider two kinds of evidence: first, the experience in the United States since 1960 for the economy as a whole in the minimum wage–unemployment relationship; and second, more micro-focused analyses of employment patterns after minimum wage changes at both the state and national level.

The U.S. Economy since 1960

Figure 2.2 examines the relationship between the declining minimum wage over time and the unemployment rate. Considering first the upper panel of the figure, we see both the unemployment rate and the minimum wage rate plotted over the time period 1960–97. It is clear that the unemployment rate does not fluctuate in the same way as the minimum wage. Indeed, if anything, the unemployment rate tends to rise throughout the 1970s and 1980s as the minimum wage falls.

This relationship becomes more clear in the lower panel of figure 2.2, in which the minimum wage and unemployment are plotted against each other. As we see from the very wide dispersion of the scatter points, there does not seem to be any close relationship between the minimum wage and unemployment. This observation is confirmed in examining the trend line, which shows the average movement in the unemployment/minimum wage relationship over our time period. We see that the trend line is actually sloping downward. This means that, if anything, the unemployment rate *goes up* when the minimum wage *goes down*—a result opposite to the view that a rising minimum wage will bring more unemployment. However, this observed downward trend is actually not a reliable observation, because the scatter points in the figure are so widely dispersed. When this happens, we cannot trust an average figure. In similar fashion, we cannot average the points per game of NBA scoring champion Michael Jordan and Robert Parish, the least productive scorer on the 1996–97 championship Chicago Bulls, and use that average to accurately describe the contributions for either Jordan or Parish. The most reliable thing we can say from such a wide array of scatter points is that there appears to be *no relationship* between unemployment and the minimum wage in this time period.

Moreover, observing this pattern over time between the movements of the minimum wage and the unem-

**Figure 2.2
Minimum Wage Rate and
Unemployment 1960-1997**

Minimum wage and unemployment trend

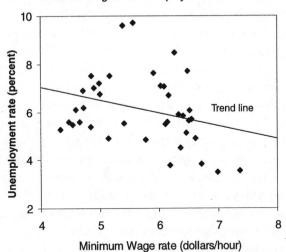

Notes: Minimum wage is in 1997 dollars. 1997 figures are through 11/97

ployment rate does not tell us anything about whether the unemployment rate is falling *as a result* of minimum wage increases, or whether there is any causal relationship at all between the two trends. But we do see that a higher minimum wage is at least *consistent with* less unemployment rather than necessarily more unemployment.

In terms of causality, one plausible explanation for what we observe in figure 2.2 is that even if a higher minimum wage did produce some unemployment if everything else in the economy were held constant, in fact, in the real world, everything else is not held constant. Other influences, such as investors, consumers, and the government demanding more goods and services could lead firms to hire more workers even if their wages are higher. Correspondingly, when demand is lower, firms would want to hire fewer workers, even if the wage at which they could hire is also lower. Such situations would therefore entail a higher minimum wage *along with* falling unemployment, and a lower minimum wage along with higher unemployment. Moreover, it is also true that Congress is more willing to raise the minimum wage when unemployment is low and wages may be rising in any case because of the tight labor market conditions. Overall then, when demand for goods and services is high, the corresponding increase in demand for workers will dominate over increases in the minimum wage in determining overall employment opportunities.

This explanation for the trend we observe is certainly consistent with the experience following the September 1997 increase in the minimum wage to $5.15 an hour amid an overall unemployment rate below 5 percent. For example, an October 27, 1997, front-page story in the *Wall Street Journal* describes the impact of the minimum wage increase on fast-food restaurants, where resistance to the raise had been intense. Titled "Chicken Feed: Minimum Wage is Up, But a Fast-Food Chain Notices Little Impact," the story reported that "the minimum wage increase has turned into one of the nonevents of 1997, thanks mostly to the economy's continuing strength. Low-wage Americans—nearly 10 million of them by some estimates—got a raise. But amid the current prosperity, hardly anybody noticed." One fast-food employer, David Rosenstein, who runs thirteen Popeyes Chicken & Biscuits restaurants in the Washington, D.C., area, had been a staunch opponent of the raise but more recently decided that "The economy is good. Business is good. . . . I think we saw it in more dire terms than it worked out."

Are Unemployment Increases Concentrated Among Low-Wage Workers?

The evidence we have considered on the minimum wage and unemployment considers unemployment for the labor market as a whole. In fact, as noted above, only 8.9 percent of the workforce actually earns the minimum wage. So perhaps we can observe the positive relationship—unemployment going up when the minimum wage goes up, and vice versa—for the segment of the labor market that actually gets minimum wage jobs. To consider this possibility, figure 2.3 looks again at the relationship between the minimum wage rate and unemployment, except that instead of showing overall unemployment data, it reports the unemployment rate for teenagers only.

It is important to emphasize in considering the teenage unemployment–minimum wage relationship that we are by no means suggesting that only teenagers, or even mainly teenagers, get paid minimum wages. Quite the contrary: as we reported above, 71

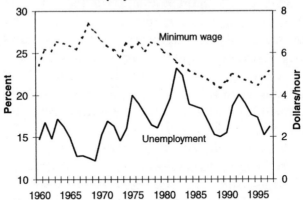

Figure 2.3
Minimum Wage Rate and Teenage
Unemployment 1960-1997

Minimum Wage and Teenage unemployment trend

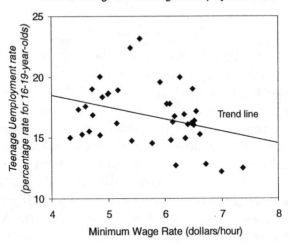

Notes: Minimum wage is in 1997 dollars. 1997 figures are through 11/97

percent of the people receiving raises through the 1996–97 minimum wage increase were not teenagers. Nevertheless, 50 percent of all teenagers who work earn the minimum wage, while only 6.8 percent of working adults have minimum wage jobs. Therefore, by considering the relationship between teenage unemployment and the minimum wage, we get a closer look at how changes in the minimum wage affect employment opportunities.

In fact, as figure 2.3 shows, the relationship between the minimum wage and teenage unemployment closely follows that for the overall unemployment rate. That is, if anything, we again see an inverse relationship—teenage unemployment went up while the minimum wage went down. But once again, the scatter of points around the trend line in the lower panel is widely dispersed. This means that there is no predictable relationship between teenage unemployment and the minimum wage over our time period, once everything else in the economy is also allowed to affect the teenage unemployment rate.

THE MINIMUM WAGE AND PRODUCTIVITY GROWTH

The fall in the real value of the minimum wage since 1968 is all the more remarkable considering that, as of 1997, the productivity of the U.S. economy—our ability to produce goods and services with a given number of people employed and given dollar value of machines—is 52 percent higher than it was in 1968. Consider a simple exercise, the results of which are reported in figure 2.4. Suppose that the minimum wage had not been dropping all these years since 1968, but rather had been rising at a rate exactly equal to the economy's rate of productivity increase. This

Figure 2.4
The Minimum Wage and Productivity

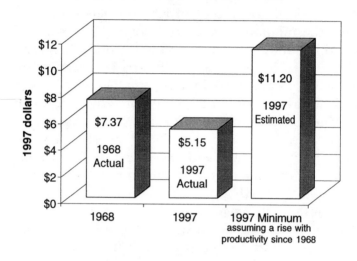

Note: 1997 Inflation figures are through 11/97.
1997 productivity figures are through 9/97.

would mean that the minimum wage would go up only when the economy could produce more goods and services in an hour's time than it could the previous year. In figure 2.4, we see that if this were the case, the minimum wage in 1997 would have been $11.20, more than double the actual $5.15 rate in 1997. This is a remarkable result. The fact that the minimum wage would be $11.20 in 1997 if low-wage workers had received only an equal share of the economy's productivity gains since 1968—no more and no less—makes certain that the productive potential exists in the economy of 1998 to sustain a significantly higher minimum wage.

CASE STUDIES ON MINIMUM
WAGE LAWS

The best-known recent analysis of this type was done by the labor economists David Card of the University of California–Berkeley and Alan Krueger of Princeton University, especially in their highly influential 1995 book *Myth and Measurement: The New Economics of the Minimum Wage.* Among their many innovative investigations, they studied the substantial 18.8 percent increase—from \$4.25 to \$5.05—in the minimum wage in 1992 for New Jersey, comparing employment after the increase with that in neighboring Pennsylvania, where the minimum wage did not change. They found that employment increased slightly more, on average, in New Jersey than in the Pennsylvania control group. This again contradicted the idea that a rise in the minimum wage rate will create employment losses, even when the rate increase is as high as the New Jersey 18.8 percent rise. At the same time, because the employment increase in New Jersey was only slightly larger, they could not conclude with confidence that the rise in the minimum wage was positively associated with increases in employment.[7]

Numerous other studies, examining the detailed changes in specific labor markets throughout the country due to an increase in the minimum wage, have produced results similar to those in Card and Krueger's analysis of New Jersey and Pennsylvania. Some of the places examined in these other studies include California before and after the 1988 increase in the state minimum wage; and the fast food industries in Texas, Jackson, Mississippi and Greensboro, North Carolina, before and after the 1992 increase in the federal minimum wage.[8]

PREVAILING WAGE LAWS
IN CONSTRUCTION

The experiences with the Davis-Bacon prevailing wage laws in the construction industry provide another useful perspective for evaluating the potential impact of living wage ordinances. As noted above, the prevailing wage laws, unlike the national and state minimum wage laws but like most living wage proposals, apply only to a small segment of the working population in a region—in this case, construction industry employees working under government contracts. Also like most living wage proposals, Davis-Bacon laws set wage floors that are well above the national and state minimum wage. However, Davis-Bacon laws do not create an invariant wage floor for its affected group but rather set wage floors according to the wage rate "prevailing" in a region.

According to the comprehensive work of Prof. Peter Phillips and colleagues at the University of Utah, major long-term benefits have resulted from both the federal and state Davis-Bacon laws.[9] First, Davis-Bacon laws have forced all companies to adhere to the same wage, benefit, and workplace standards when they compete for government contracts. This standardization of compensation levels and workplace conditions allows construction work to be a solid career for working people. In addition, the fact that workers receive decent wages has meant that investment in training is encouraged either through employers or unions. These industry training standards provide avenues for less-skilled, less-educated workers to acquire the skills they need to have stable, decently paid working lives.

In addition, responsible, higher-paying contractors can now compete successfully with contractors who seek to obtain contracts through driving down wages and "lowball" bidding. Creating a level playing field for such contractors has also encouraged high safety standards in the construction industry, which is, in any case, one of the most dangerous industries in the U.S. economy.

The encouragement of skilled labor and relatively high wages has also meant that, in general, the quality of the work done by government contractors is high. Contractors that compete through low bidding are much more apt to allow an unsafe workplace, poorer quality work, and expensive cost overruns. Finally, because of the wage, benefit, and safety standards established by Davis-Bacon, construction workers are taxpayers contributing to the public treasury, rather than drawing on public funds for food stamps, public health support, and low-income tax credits.

EFFECTS OF "LITTLE DAVIS-BACON" REPEALS

Nine states repealed their "little Davis-Bacon Acts" between 1979 and 1988. These actions provide a good "before and after" laboratory for observing the effects of prevailing wage legislation.

The effects of repeal on earnings, employment, and overall incomes in the construction industry have been estimated in detail by Prof. Phillips and colleagues. In table 2.1, we present a simplified but realistic model that illustrates the main findings of the Phillips study.

For simplicity, our model assumes that the total number of construction workers in our hypothetical state is 1000, of which 900 are initially employed and 100 are unemployed. Other than this one simplification, the values used in the model are close approxi-

Table 2.1

Model of "Little Davis-Bacon" Repeals
on Incomes, Employment, and State Revenues

(Assumes state has 1,000 construction workers
with a 10% unemployment rate)

	Before Repeal	After Repeal	Net Effect	Percentage Effect
Construction Income	$25,000	$23,500	-$1,500	-6%
Construction Employment	900 Employed 100 Unemployed	918 Employed 82 Unemployed	+18 Jobs	+1.8%
Total Incomes in Construction	$22.5 million	$21.6 million	-$900,000	-4.0%
Total State Revenue[a]	$2.7 million	$2.6 million	-$100,000	-4.0%

[a]Calculated with a 7 percent income tax and 5 percent sales tax, with worker consuming all of income.

mations to the actual figures reported by Phillips and colleagues.

To begin with, we see in table 2.1 that the average annual income of a construction worker is $25,000 before the Davis-Bacon repeal, but drops by 6.0 percent, to $23,500, as a result of the repeal. This fall in incomes does bring more employment in construction. Eighteen more jobs are created, which leads to a 1.8 percent decline in the unemployment rate in construction, from 10 percent to 8.2 percent. However, at least in part, this decline in the unemployment rate may be attributable to people dropping out of the job market after wages have declined in construction—in other words, *unemployment rate declines* may be greater than the *employment gains*.

Note that on a percentage basis, the decline in each employed construction worker's income of 6 percent is greater than the fall in the unemployment rate of 1.8 percent. We see the effect of these disproportional changes in the figures for total incomes in construction, which fell from $22.5 to $21.6 million. This is a 4 percent decline in the overall incomes of construction workers. Finally, such a decline in incomes translates into a comparable decline in state income and sales taxes. In our model, the state loses $100,000 in revenue, or 4 percent of its budget, due to the Davis-Bacon repeal. The overall revenue loss depends on the proportion that construction workers' income represents relative to that for the entire state.

In addition to these considerations, Phillips and colleagues report three other major effects from the repeal of the little Davis-Bacons: (1) Spending on training for a new generation of construction workers fell by 40 percent; (2) Minority representation in construction training programs fell even faster than the 40 percent overall drop in training, thus creating severe difficulties for workers with minority back-grounds to pursue a career in construction;[10] and (3) Occupational injuries in construction rose by 15 per-cent.

In short, we do observe some rise in construction employment after the state Davis-Bacon laws were re-pealed. But these job increases come at a stiff price: declines in overall incomes and state revenue; far fewer training opportunities, especially for minorities, and a significantly less safe work environment. Thus, it is clear that Davis-Bacon has had a major positive im-pact for workers in the construction industry, espe-cially for young people and minorities. The employment gains through repeal are not inconse-quential. But it is important to emphasize again the evidence that unemployment rates, even for teenag-ers, do not depend primarily on changes in the mini-mum wage. They are rather set by broader economic factors, such as the overall level of demand in the economy for goods and services.

THE INITIAL BALTIMORE EXPERIENCE WITH MUNICIPAL LIVING WAGE

The Baltimore living wage ordinance, the first such law in the country, went into effect in July 1995, es-tablishing a minimum wage of $6.10 per hour for any-one working on a city contract. The living wage ordinance stipulates that the wage be increased annu-ally, upon approval by the city's Board of Estimates, aiming by 1999 to equal the amount required to raise a family of four above the poverty line. The minimum wage has thus been raised by increments, to $6.60 in July 1996 and to $7.10 in July 1997. By 1999, the wage is to reach $7.70, the level at which a full-time worker's pay equals about 90 percent of the four-person-family poverty threshold. At that point, the minimum wage is to be indexed to inflation so that it stays about 10 percent below the four-person family poverty threshold.

The Baltimore living wage ordinance faced strong opposition from the local business community. They made the familiar arguments that the living wage would increase costs to the city, reduce the number of bidders on city contracts, and force city contractors to lay off workers.

In October 1996, Mark Weisbrot and Michelle Sforza-Roderick of the Washington, D.C.–based Preamble Center for Public Policy published *Baltimore's Living Wage Law,* a careful study of the effects of the Baltimore ordinance. Their analysis focused on contracts whose labor costs have increased or are expected to increase as a result of the living wage ordinance. The City's Bureau of Management and Budget Research provided them with a list of the types of contracts that would be affected by the ordinance, as well as the dollar amount of all the contracts. The Bureau determined that, as of December 1995, the total value of contracts falling under the wage requirement was $26.8 million. Weisbrot and Sforza-Roderick obtained full or partial information on 46 contracts involving 75 companies; others had not yet been rebid under the living wage requirements. Those contracts that have been rebid since the passage of the living wage ordinance and for which information on contract amounts and bidding patterns was available are presented in table 2.2. The value of the 46 contracts they studied is $19.3 million, amounting to 72 percent of the total value of those contracts affected by the ordinance.

Amounts of winning bids. The third and fourth columns of table 2.2 report post–living wage changes in the winning bid amounts both without adjusting for inflation (i.e., in "current" dollars) and after making

Table 2.2

City of Baltimore Contract Bidding Patterns Before and After 1996 Living Wage Ordinance

Contract Name	Amount of Winning Bids				Number of Bids	
	Pre–Living Wage (current dollars)	Post–Living Wage (current dollars)	Post–Living Wage (inflation-adjusted dollars)		Pre–Living Wage	Post–Living Wage
Public pupil bus transportation	14.14 million	14.50 million	14.21 million		NA	NA
Commission on aging nutritional meals	2.52 million	2.16 million	2.05 million		3	2
Summer food service program for youth	1.29 million	1.33 million	1.30 million		1	1
General charter bus service	750,000	750,000	709,917		18	17
Homemaker/personal care services	268,400	258,280	246,192		4	5
General moving and hauling	118,650	118,508	112,623		5	4
Homemaker services	72,000	84,528	80,171		4	5
Grass cutting	44,604	31,500	30,693		4	4
Camp variety bus transportation	30,000	35,440	32,654		7	3
Athletic and cultural bus transportation	NA	NA	NA		23	15

Hauling of voting machines	NA	NA	NA	2	2
Maintenance and repairs on trailers	NA	NA	NA	2	1
Janitorial Contracts					
A)	21,372	18,456	17,400	15	13
B)	10,068	12,000	11,325	NA	NA
C)	9,600	10,128	9,510	NA	NA
D)	9,600	7,312	6,873	1	2
E)	8,100	8,400	7,364	NA	NA
F)	8,010	8,700	8,210	NA	NA
G)	7,346	7,313	6,887	NA	NA
H)	6,672	8,000	7,342	NA	NA
I)	5,940	8,736	8,244	NA	NA
J)	5,628	7,616	7,173	°NA	NA
Totals	**$19.33 million**	**$19.37 million** (= 0.2% increase)	**$18.86 million** (= 2.4% total decline; 1.9% average decline per contract)	**93** (= 6.6 bids per contract)	**76** (= 5.4 bids per contract)

NOTE: "NA" means not available

an appropriate adjustment for inflation. As we see with the total figures presented in the bottom row of the table, in current dollars the total value of the winning bids rose from $19.33 million to $19.37 million, an increase of 0.2 percent. Measured in inflation-adjusted dollars, the total post–living wage winning bids actually *fell* to $18.86 million, a decline of 2.4 percent. Because the individual contracts reported in table 2.2 vary so greatly in amount—ranging between $14.5 million and $7,300—it is also important to measure how much each winning contract bid might have changed before and after implementation of the living wage ordinance. As we see in the bottom row, this change in inflation-adjusted terms was, on average, a 1.9 percent decline in the winning bid amounts.

What could account for this result, given that at least some of the contractors in this sample faced an increase in their labor costs as a result of the living wage? The most likely explanation, again, is that other factors overwhelmed the impact of these cost increases. From interviews with contractors, Weisbrot and Sforza-Roderick found that firms commonly try to underbid the previous year's contract. Standard competitive pressures of the bidding process may therefore have forced firms to absorb their increased costs due to the living wage ordinance. This is probably true for the food and bus contractors, who reported that they did not adjust their bids for the increased labor costs. Most janitorial companies reported that they did in fact take the increased labor costs into account when formulating their bids, but these increases did not show up in the overall costs of the new contracts.

We cannot, of course, conclude that the living wage ordinance actually contributed to lowering the cost of the average contract. However, as we discuss at length in chapter 5, firms can experience efficiency gains through paying higher wages, particularly in the form of lower turnover and absenteeism by workers once they begin to earn a decent wage. This factor could have lowered firms' costs. Weisbrot and Sforza-Roderick report that in telephone interviews with the contractors, many did in fact stress that paying higher wages reduced turnover. For example, one of the larger janitorial contractors, who said he always paid more than the federal minimum, states that at wages below $5.00 an hour the problems of turnover and absenteeism were too large.

Fewer than 1,000 workers were impacted through the first round of Baltimore's living wage increases. (Because of the limited monitoring of the ordinance by the city, no official figures exist on how many workers have been affected.) So even if contract costs had increased by the full amount of the potential increase in labor costs, the impact on Baltimore's $2 billion budget would have been slight. However, even these very small increases in the cost of city contracts did not materialize from the evidence assembled by Weisbrot and Sforza-Roderick.

Impact on Bidding Practices. The last two columns of table 2.2 show figures on the number of bids for each of the contracts affected by the living wage. As we see there, Weisbrot and Sforza-Roderick were unable to obtain information on bidding patterns for 9 of the 23 contracts reported in the table, including that for the largest contract, "Public Pupil Bus Transportation," as well as for most of the janitorial contracts. Considering the 14 contracts on which information was obtained, in eight cases the number of bids fell while in six cases the number of bids increased or stayed the same. The average number of bids per contract fell from 6.6 to 5.4, but the janitorial contract buyer for the city told Weisbrot and Sforza-Roderick that this change was well within the normal range by which numbers of bidders fluctuate in any given year.

So, overall, critics who insisted that the living wage ordinance would reduce the number of bids on city contracts were wrong. Indeed, Weisbrot and Sforza-Roderick found that the contractors themselves were generally positive about the effects of the living wage ordinance on bidding. The prevailing opinion offered was that the living wage "levels the playing field" and relieved pressure on employers to squeeze labor costs in order to win low-bid contracts. A bus company manager said that "we feel more able to compete against businesses who were drastically reducing wages in order to put in a low bid." If more firms think they have a chance to win city service contracts because of the living wage requirement, the number of bidders could actually increase over time.

Impact on Contractor Employment Levels. Have contractors responded to increased labor costs by laying off workers or by failing to hire as many as they otherwise would have? For the most part, direct payroll figures were not available to Weisbrot and Sforza-Roderick. Thus, to determine whether the increased labor costs resulted in reduced employment, Weisbrot and Sforza-Roderick interviewed those contractors who held a contract both before and after the ordinance went into effect and whose labor costs increased as a result of the ordinance. This sample consisted of 31 companies, including providers of transportation, janitorial, food and administrative services.

None of the companies interviewed reported any reduction in staff levels to compensate for the increased cost of labor resulting from the living wage requirement. For example, the city's janitorial contracts have the highest percentage of costs attributable to low-wage labor. Of the two janitorial companies holding pre- and post-ordinance contracts, neither reported reducing staff levels to compensate for the increased costs. In addition, the large janitorial contracts, those for schools, have mandatory staff levels set by the city that could not be altered in response to the living wage requirements.

The $14.5 million school bus contract—actually a multiple contract with 26 companies that accounts for 75 percent of the $19.4 total for all post–living wage winning contract bids—demonstrates clearly the difficulties that contractors will frequently face if they wish to reduce staffing levels in response to the living wage requirements. Outside of office overhead, the labor force for bus contracts consists entirely of bus drivers and aides, the aides being required on special-needs buses for elderly citizens and the disabled. To cut staffing in this case would therefore entail direct cuts in services provided.

Overall then, from nearly two years' experience with the living wage in Baltimore, the negative effects predicted by its opponents did not materialize. The winning bids on city contracts increased only slightly in current dollars and actually decreased in inflation-adjusted dollars. The number of bidders for the contracts in our sample did decline, but not by a significant amount. Finally, interviews with contractors indicated that they did not reduce their workforce in response to the living wage.

It will take more time and further research to obtain a fuller understanding of how contractors in Baltimore have responded to the living wage ordinance, and how their responses affect employment, productivity, and costs to the city government. But through nearly two years since the ordinance was enacted, the claims of living wage opponents—that it would increase unemployment and raise costs to the city—were not borne out.

3—Living Wages and Urban Development Policies

L iving wage campaigns have emerged primarily at the level of municipal governments. There are several reasons why this has happened. As a matter of strategic politics, living wage campaigns have a greater chance of success in municipalities than at the state or national level since at the municipal level the power of big-money politics is still lower. This is true, even though it is also the case that in most municipalities, business interests have mounted expensive campaigns to defeat these measures.

There is a second obvious, if less strategic reason why these campaigns have been focused on municipalities. This is because the problem of poverty and low-wage employment are severe in the cities. As of 1996, there were more than 16 million city residents living in poverty—nearly 20 percent of the country's city-dwelling population. This was more than double the rate for those living in suburbs. The situation for families with children under 18 is worse still—more than 25 percent of these city-dwelling families are impoverished, as opposed to 11 percent of families in suburbs with children. These problems of urban poverty and low-wage employment will be exacerbated as the effects of ending federal welfare assistance spread. Abolishing federal welfare support will bring more job-seekers into the low-wage labor market, and as such, it will also exert downward pressure on wages. If policy is to be focused on getting people off government assistance and into employment, establishing a living wage minimum is the most concrete step governments can take to prevent this increase in low-wage job-seekers from worsening the conditions of urban poverty.

Then there is a third important reason why the living wage campaigns have emerged in municipalities. Since at least the early 1980s, municipal governments, in conjunction with states and the federal government, have pursued an active agenda for reversing the economic decline of cities. "Urban development" is the term broadly applied to these efforts. What this has meant in practice is that governments have actively sought to attract businesses to locate within their cities through offering them a wide array of subsidies and other enticements. Much political capital, and more importantly, huge financial resources, have been devoted to these efforts. However, an overall examination of the evidence makes clear that these policies have failed to reduce urban poverty and reverse the decline of urban communities, even when, as is the case in some cities, these policies have promoted the growth of downtown businesses.

Living wage policies—and the campaigns to make such policies a reality—represent an important challenge to the business subsidy model of urban development. Certainly, living wage policies cannot stand by themselves as a full-fledged alternative to the business subsidy approach. But they should be seen as a crucial component of any broader alternative policy framework. First of all, no matter what else a municipal government may seek to do to alleviate its city's social problems, the living wage policy makes a clear statement that the final goal of any program should be decent jobs for its residents. All policy initiatives can then be judged according to how effective they will be in promoting living wage jobs. Also, establishing a living wage standard makes clear the types of business firms that the city is trying to attract, retain, or promote. Not all businesses will make positive contributions to the social development of cities; and in particular, those firms that are unwilling to pay living wages are not the types of firms on which cities should be showering their scarce resources. Finally, the political effort to establish a living wage policy requires community mobilization. Once the community is mobilized around the living wage, broader questions will also arise as to both the ends and means of urban development. In short, the fight for a living wage policy will inevitably generate new debates about urban development policies among segments of the community that may have previously neglected such questions.

Given these considerations, it will be useful here to review the experiences with the urban development policies that have prevailed since the early 1980s. We will consider estimates of their costs, and then evaluate their benefits according to three criteria: their impact on economic growth within the targeted municipality; their success in generating new jobs; and the contributions they make to promoting the equitable distribution of income and public services. Finally, we will consider some alternatives to the business subsidy model that have been emerging recently.

BUSINESS SUBSIDIES FOR URBAN DEVELOPMENT

The basic premise of the business subsidy strategy as it developed through the 1980s is straightforward. It is that as middle-class populations left the cities for the suburbs in the post–World War II era, the cities became increasingly unattractive places to do business. Compounding this problem was the fact that businesses were becoming more mobile in an era of sophisticated communication and transportation technologies. They could move almost anywhere in search of better profit opportunities. In particular, according to this perspective, businesses will seek locations where wage rates and taxes are low.

Thus, the task for municipal governments was straightforward: to keep business costs to a minimum in their city. The most direct way to do this was to offer financial subsidies and related forms of support to businesses they wanted to attract to the city. Once the city governments succeeded in attracting businesses through this strategy, the businesses would presumably create new jobs and higher tax revenues for the city. According to proponents of this urban development approach, this is how subsidies to business end up creating broadly shared benefits for all sectors of the city.

This business subsidy strategy was most forcefully articulated in the influential 1981 book *City Limits* (University of Chicago Press) by the University of Chicago political scientist Paul Peterson. But as a matter of practical policy, state governments in Alabama and Mississippi first experimented with such policies as far back as the 1940s. Municipal government officials in various parts of the country began implementing this approach in the early 1970s. Thus, Peter Eisinger recounts in his book *The Rise of the Entreprenurial State* that newly elected African American mayors were among the most enthusiastic supporters of such policies. Examining the transition to black mayoralties in Atlanta and Detroit in the mid-1970s, Eisinger writes that

I was struck at the time that a major way both mayors, May-nard Jackson [Atlanta] and Coleman Young [Detroit], at-tempted to reach out to white elites was to promote private investment opportunities, mostly in the downtowns of their cities. That the mayors in these cities concentrated so avidly on commercial construction in their respective central busi-ness districts had a certain irony in these racially divided cities. Yet both men justified their attentiveness to what were overwhelmingly white interests by arguing that the jobs and tax revenues generated by these projects would benefit their black constituents both directly and indirectly.[1]

The business subsidy approach to municipal devel-opment is also closely tied to the economic policy ideas that rose dramatically into ascendancy in the late 1970s and early 1980s throughout much of the world, including Latin America, the former Communist countries of Eastern Europe, the United States, and the United Kingdom. The terms used for such policies became familiar—Reaganism, Thatcherism, neoliber-alism, supply-side economics, and, less approvingly, trickle-down economics. But under whatever name, the principle is the same: the primary role the govern-ment should play in promoting economic success is to do everything possible to create a favorable business climate. In practice this has meant minimizing busi-ness taxes, regulations, public ownership of enter-prises, and policy interventions to reduce unemployment. It has also meant restricting the power of unions and other organized forces that can threaten to raise wages or impose other barriers to business success. Proponents of such policies believe that businesses thrive when such a climate exists, and when businesses thrive, benefits flow—or "trickle down"—to all segments of society. The effects of such policies—and the allied "shock therapy" interventions and "structural adjustment" programs of the Interna-tional Monetary Fund and World Bank—are no longer matters of dispute: they produced slower growth and often depression-level contractions; a more concentrated distribution of income and wealth; and more widespread unemployment and poverty.[2] Nevertheless, such policies are still favored in orthodox circles because, whatever else they achieve, they are certain to yield benefits to the already privileged.

Within U.S. cities themselves, the business subsidy approach takes a wide variety of forms. The most commonly used incentive by cities as well as state governments is some kind of tax reduction, or "abatement." As Greg LeRoy writes in his 1994 study *No More Candy Stores*, "Tax credit programs have proliferated so that states and cities now abate or credit almost every kind of corporate tax they collect: property and real estate tax, inventory, sales, corporate income and utility taxes. They may also grant accelerated depreciation or tax credits for special activities such as research and development."[3]

Enterprise zones, or what the Clinton Administration calls "empowerment zones" are the best-known and most widely used form of tax abatement in cities. The establishment of the empowerment zone program in 1993 has been the most ambitious urban policy initiative of the Clinton administration. In somewhat different forms, enterprise zone policies had been implemented beginning in the 1980s by a wide range of state and local governments. As a federal program, the idea had been discussed actively, though never passed into law, in both the Reagan and Bush administrations. Jack Kemp, the Secretary of Housing and Urban Development under Bush, and Bob Dole's running mate in the 1996 presidential election, has long been the most vocal proponent of enterprise zones among prominent U.S. politicians.

What is an enterprise zone? LeRoy describes them as follows:

> Typically a zone will include several acres of urban land gerrymandered into an irregular shape to include both blighted areas and, often, properties owned by politically-connected companies. For companies located in the zone or who move into it, several kinds of tax breaks are offered. Usually, local property or real estate taxes are abated for a set number of years, then phased back in. The company may be given a state corporate income tax credit for each person it hires. The company may also get excused from state inventory taxes on its working stock, on state sales tax for its new equipment and/or its raw materials, and from income taxes, if there are any.[4]

Direct financial support for businesses often come in the form of Industrial Development Bonds (IDB), government sponsored bonds whose proceeds go to a company for its investment. The companies benefit because they are able to obtain a loan at a rate below that which they would have obtained on the private market. Other types of economic development grants available to support private businesses in urban areas are Community Development Block Grants, Economic Development Administration Grants, Tax Increment Financing Districts (TIF), and, until 1989, Urban Development Action Grants (UDAG). Details aside, each of these programs are vehicles for cities and states to provide subsidies that attract businesses to their localities.

These programs are widespread among cities and states. Considering enterprise zone programs alone, thirty-four states had some form of active program in place as of 1995. Among municipalities, with the enactment of the Clinton Administration's Federal Empowerment Zone and Enterprise Community Program, the enterprise zone concept was extended to

106 additional communities. All 50 states have pursued some type of IDB financing initiative as of 1996.

How Much Do Business Subsidy Programs Cost?

Remarkably, little systematic evidence exists as to how much these programs actually cost. Few states or cities keep track of how much they forego in lost tax revenues through abatements, credits, and other forms of "tax expenditures" targeted for economic development. Even fewer states or cities monitor the performance of companies that are granted subsidies. For example, a business may promise to create some large number of jobs in exchange for a tax abatement, but the government granting the abatement does not normally follow up to determine whether the promised jobs were ever actually created.

Despite this lack of official accounting, various cost estimates of these programs do exist. There is strong evidence, for example, that, measured relative to the number of jobs promised by a business, the amounts municipalities are giving away in tax dollars to attract businesses has been rising sharply since the early 1980s. A 1989 study by H. Brinton Milward and Heidi Hosbach Newman, for example, estimated costs through the 1980s of financial incentives awarded to automobile manufacturers as location incentives. They found that, in 1980, Nissan received about $11,000 for each new promised job to locate in Symrna, Tennessee. By 1984, Mazda got an estimated $13,857 per promised job for locating in Flat Rock, Michigan. Milward and Newman's estimates of tax concessions for each promised job then rise as follows: Saturn, $26,667 per job in 1985 to locate in Spring Hill, Tennessee; Diamond-Star, $33,320 per job in 1985 to locate in Bloomington-Normal, Illinois; Toyota, $49,900 per job in 1985 to locate in Georgetown, Kentucky; and Fuji-Isuzu, $50,588 per job in 1989 to locate in Lafayette, Indiana. The pattern of rising costs per promised job appears to have only intensified since the period studied by Milward and Newman. When BMW chose to locate in South Carolina in 1992, the tax concessions they obtained per promised job amounted to an estimated $68,421. By 1993, Mercedez Benz was persuaded to locate just outside Birmingham, Alabama, at an estimated subsidy of about $168,000 per promised job.[5]

Beyond these specific cases of subsidies, it is more difficult to obtain a comprehensive picture of the amounts government forego to attract businesses. The most reliable figures are for federal government programs alone, and even here, no firm figures exist. The congressional Joint Committee on Taxation produces estimates of all forms of relief—or "tax expenditures"—provided in the federal tax laws, and these include estimates for Industrial Development Bonds and, more recently, enterprise zone programs.

In table 3.1, we report the Taxation Committee's estimates on foregone revenue for the years 1981–2000 for the Industrial Revenue Bond and the years 1996–2000 for the enterprise zone program. For the years 1996–2000, we also provide alternative estimates of the same IDB and enterprise zone programs by Citizens for Tax Justice, the respected Washington research institute. As we see from the upper left-hand panel of the table, the Taxation Committee estimates average revenue losses from Industrial Development Bond programs at $2.6 billion per year between 1991 and 1995. This figure is well below that for 1986–90, but nevertheless, still represents a sizable share of the government's total commitment to developing urban areas. It is nearly equal to the $3.0 billion per year the federal government spent on urban mass transit from

Table 3.1

Federal Tax Revenues Foregone through Industrial Development Bonds and Enterprise Zone Programs

Industrial Development Bonds

Estimate	Joint Taxation Committee Estimate	Citizens for Tax Justice
1981–85	$2.4 billion/year	—
1986–90	$3.2 billion/year	—
1991–95	$2.6 billion/year	—
1996–2000	$0.666 billion/year	$0.90 billion/year

Enterprise Zones

1996–2000	$0.56 billion/year	$0.48 billion/year

Sources: Staff of the Joint Committee on Taxation, "Estimates of Federal Tax Expenditures," various years; Citizens for Tax Justice, *The Hidden Entitlements*, May 1996.

1991 to 1995, and is 62 percent of total federal outlays of $4.2 billion on physical investments for community and regional development.

From 1996 to 2000, the Taxation Committee estimates that the Industrial Development Bond program will fall again, to $666 million per year, a substantial cut resulting from the balanced federal budget agreement reached in Congress in 1997. Again, however, $666 million is still a full 14 percent of the total Housing and Urban Development's $4.8 billion average annual expenditures between 1996 and 2000 for grants to state and local governments.

But we also see in table 3.1 that the Citizens for Tax Justice has estimated lost revenue between 1996 and 2000 for the Industrial Bond Program at $900 million, 35 percent higher than that of the Taxation Committee. Without getting into the details of the alternative methodologies, the important point illustrated is that a substantial degree of ambiguity exists in calculating revenue lost through such tax-concession programs. The government's own figures cannot be taken as necessarily hard and fast, which is hardly a satisfactory state of affairs when we are dealing with billions of dollars annually in public subsidies to business. Moreover, if we applied the Citizens for Tax Justice methodology for the 1981–95 figures, we would find that the total tax revenues forgone would again be about 35 percent higher. This would mean that the money foregone from Industrial Revenue Bonds was now greater, for example, than total federal spending on urban mass transit.

Table 3.1 also shows estimates of both the Joint Taxation Committee and Citizens for Tax Justice of revenues lost through the enterprise zone program between 1996 and 2000. Here the two sets of estimates are fairly close, ranging between an average of

$480–$560 million per year. And these figures do not include the tax revenues foregone at the state or municipal levels, where the more substantial enterprise zone programs have operated since the early 1980s.

In addition, in reporting these figures for Industrial Development Bonds and Enterprise Zones, we have hardly skimmed the surface of the array of subsidy programs available to businesses through tax relief. For example, we have not included all the tax-free bond subsidy programs that could be considered as part of a region's strategy for attracting businesses. Just one additional budgetary item of this type is the issuance of bonds to finance airports, docks, and sports and convention facilities. Between 1996 and 2000, these subsidies are estimated to total another $1.3 to $1.8 billion per year in foregone federal tax revenue.

The overall point then is clear: considering policies at the federal level alone, government programs are providing formidable subsidies to businesses to promote urban development. State and local policies have been pursuing similar agendas. However else one might judge these programs, one glaring problem is that we don't even have firm figures as to how much these efforts cost. We know the amount is in the billions annually, but beyond this, the direct accounting for costs ranges from being incomplete to nonexistent across various government bodies. Without a clear understanding of costs, it is difficult to assess whether the benefits of the programs justify their costs. However, it is crucial that such benefit-to-cost comparisons be made.

Benefits of Business Subsidy Programs

The lack of adequate accounting for costs of business subsidy programs is paralleled by large gaps in the information needed to assess their benefits. In almost no cases do states or municipalities have formal procedures for estimating the impact of these programs according to some clear set of criteria. Indeed, in most cases, the award of subsidies by firms is not conditional on the firms meeting any specified obligations. In other words, governments grant subsidies to businesses on the businesses' promise of various benefits they will provide to a city or state. But, as noted above, rarely do governments ever determine whether such benefits amounted to more than just promises.

Nevertheless, a substantial literature does by now exist that estimates what the benefits are of these programs. We consider them in terms their impact on economic growth, on jobs, and on the distribution of income and public services.

Economic Growth

Despite differences in details, the primary tool governments employ for promoting economic growth in their region is some form of business tax reduction. But do these tax reductions in fact promote economic growth?

A 1997 article by Syracuse University economics professor Michael Wasylenko in the *New England Economic Review* addresses just this question. Prof. Wasylenko surveyed approximately seventy-five recent research papers that have examined various aspects of this question.[6] The results of this body of research vary considerably, as should be expected, given that there are significant differences in the way a researcher can approach the question at hand. For example, in looking at the impact of tax reductions on a region's "economic growth," do we consider income growth, employment growth, new business investment, business relocations, new business creations, or some other category as the target measure of "economic growth"? Wasylenko finds that the conclusions one draws about development policies will vary according to which target one chooses to examine, and also according to other criteria.

Nevertheless, Wasylenko draws some general conclusions based on the weight of the overall evidence. His first important conclusion is that, everything else being equal, a city or state that lowers its taxes will succeed in promoting economic growth in a sometimes small, but almost always significant way relative to its neighboring localities that have higher taxes. To be more specific, if the state of Arizona were to lower its business taxes by 10 percent relative to those for California, the evidence suggests businesses will grow in Arizona about 2 percent faster than they do in California. In the case of relative tax rates among neighboring cities within a larger region, the impact of reducing business taxes is likely to be much larger. Thus, if Los Angeles were to lower its business taxes by 10 percent relative to Pasadena, Santa Monica, and Compton, LA businesses will grow faster than those in neighboring cities by as much as 8 to 9 percent.

However, as Wasylenko emphasizes, these positive benefits to a tax reduction strategy are completely dependent not just on one city or state lowering its business taxes. *It is also necessary that neighboring localities not lower their own business taxes as well.* When other localities do also lower their taxes, the benefits of this strategy to any given locality are lost.

Some important implications follow from this last point. First, it means that whether cutting business taxes will in fact promote economic growth will vary tremendously over time and between regions. In the 1970s, some locations were successful in generating growth through this strategy because other govern-

ments had not yet fully understood the need to respond in kind. But by the 1980s, governments
throughout the United States almost universally recognized the dynamics of the tax-cutting strategy.
Moreover, by the 1980s foreign governments as well
began to enter the tax-cutting competition to attract
U.S. firms and those from other countries. As a result,
most of the studies reviewed by Wasylenko found that
the tax-cutting strategy was much more successful in
the 1970s than subsequently.

By the 1980s, what has come to be known as the
"war between the states" had escalated to a phase of
heavy mutual bloodletting. In many cases, the costs of
winning the war had risen so high that victory was no
longer worth the price of fighting. We observed this
dynamic through the cost escalation in seeking to attract auto manufacturing plants between 1980 and
1993 — $11,000 per promised job to land Nissan in
1980; $168,000 per promised job to get Mercedes-
Benz in 1993. Even after adjusting for inflation, this
represents an extraordinary 771 percent increase in
the cost per job state and local governments are willing to pay to attract businesses.

Examining the period since 1980s as a whole, Wasylenko concludes that this escalating war between localities through tax cutting has in fact led to the
nullification of its benefits. He writes that

> taxes do not appear to have substantial effect on economic
> activity among states. In part, states and regions have acted
> to neutralize the effect of taxes by adopting tax systems that
> are more alike. Without significant differences in state tax
> systems, *taxes will not play a significant role in firm location and
> expansion.*[7]

Impact on Jobs

One way to assess the impact of these programs on
economic growth is to focus on their impact on em-

ployment. Do business subsidy programs lead to the growth of jobs in an area? The considerations we have just reviewed in terms of economic growth are again the central concern. That is, we first want to know whether business subsidies will create jobs in a locality. If they do, we then need to ask how much governments are paying to businesses to create these jobs. We also want to know whether more jobs have actually been created within a broader region, or whether one locality has just poached away the jobs from neighboring localities. If poaching is the basis for one area's employment gains, then it also follows that these gains will be nullified as soon as the other areas reciprocate with their own enticements to businesses.

As to the first, most narrow, question—whether jobs are actually created at all through the business subsidy strategy—the evidence from recent studies is mixed. On the whole, rearchers find that the business subsidy strategy does usually, though not always, bring jobs to a locality. For example, in 1993, the federal Government Accounting Office (GAO) examined the Industrial Development Bond programs in Ohio, Indiana, and New Jersey. These bonds were all issued to support projects in manufacturing—either an investment in a new manufacturing plant, the renovation of an existing plant, or the purchase of new equipment within a plant. The GAO interviewed the developers who received subsidized loans in 1991. In answering the GAO's question on what would have happened if they had not gotten government subsidized loans, 41 of the 68 developers, or 60 percent of the total, said they would have proceeded in any event. However, some of these projects would have been scaled down or experienced delays. Given all these considerations, the estimated effect of project scale-downs and cancellations is that of the 3,500 jobs that developers said their projects created, about 1,700 jobs would have been created in any event, while about 1,800 jobs would not have been created without government subsidies.

The favorable interpretation that one can therefore put on these figures is that the Industrial Development Bonds have encouraged job-creating investments. Clearly, not all the subsidies were needed for the 3,500 jobs to have been created. But at least according to the developers themselves, they would not have given jobs to about half of their new employees had the government not given them a subsidized loan.

However, this favorable interpretation is not the one the GAO itself puts on the situation. They emphasize that their own study does not say whether these 1,800 jobs are really new jobs or merely poached jobs. As they put it,

> the 1,800 jobs may not represent net new job creation, however, because this estimate does not take into account that if money were not invested in IDB projects, the money would have been used elsewhere in the economy, also creating jobs. Whether IDB financing would create more or fewer jobs than alternative investments is not known, but the result would depend on the specific alternative investment.[8]

In other words, the GAO has no idea whether these 1,800 jobs are new or poached jobs, nor are they confident that the money spent on Industrial Development Bonds was the most effective way to use government funds to stimulate job growth.

Various studies on the effects of enterprise zone programs on employment generated equally mixed findings. For example, David Dowall, a professor of city and regional planning at the University of California—Berkeley published in 1996 the first systematic, multiyear assessment of the 34 enterprise zone programs in California and concluded that they had not stimulated employment in these zones. Indeed, after accounting for overall employment growth within a given region as well as changes in the mix of industries in an area that could influence the availability of jobs, Dowall found that employment growth in California's enterprise zones was actually lower than in the non–enterprise zone areas.

Dowall acknowledges that his results differ significantly from those done for other regions. For example, he cites a study of 23 British enterprise zones which found that the zone programs had caused significant job increases. Similarly, a study of zones in New Jersey and Indiana also found significant job increases within these zones. Dowall himself concludes that "the New Jersey and British experiences suggest that when zone program incentives are economically attractive, well targeted, and effectively marketed, they can generate substantial increases in employment."[9]

The most extensive recent survey (1996) of the research on enterprise zones by professors Margaret Wilder and Barry Rubin supports Dowall's view that if the subsidies associated with zones are large enough and well targeted, these programs will generate jobs. But this conclusion then raises more questions. Are they really new jobs, or merely jobs poached from other localities? Do the jobs being created pay decently? Do they offer training opportunities? How long do they last? How much does it cost to create them? Wilder and Rubin recognize that most existing research is unable to answer these more fundamental questions; indeed, they make clear that very little effort has been made even to attempt to answer them.[10]

One serious effort to address these broader questions is a 1996 study for the Minneapolis Federal Reserve Bank by professors Peter Fisher and Alan Peters of the urban and regional planning program at the University of Iowa. Among other things, Fisher and Peters make clear what the appropriate criteria should be for measuring the overall job impact of business subsidy programs. For the country as a whole, or even a region, business subsidy programs will produce net benefits only if the programs succeed in redistributing jobs from areas of low unemployment to those suffering from high unemployment. By contrast, governments are financing mere poaching operations if the subsidies just move jobs from one low-unemployment area to another, or, for that matter, from one high-unemployment area to another.

Fisher and Peters' overall conclusion is that the various business subsidy programs throughout the country do not especially favor areas with high unemployment. Rather they find that

> after at least a decade and a half of intense competition for investment and jobs, and the widespread adoption of pro-development tax policies and development programs, states and cities have produced a system of taxes and incentives that provides no clear inducement for firms to invest in higher-unemployment places.[11]

Fisher and Peters offer two explanations for this conclusion. First, they find that high unemployment is not normally the most important reason that states and municipalities offer business incentives. More important concerns for policymakers are "slow growth" in their area, considered more broadly than just employment growth; and "simple imitation" of other states and municipalities. However, Fisher and Peters also find that even when high unemployment might have provided the initial impetus to begin offering business subsidies, the subsidies are likely to continue even after the employment situation in a given locality improves. Considering the country as a whole then, the location incentives governments offer to businesses end up having little to do with the employment problems of any given area.

Overall then, we do see some increases in jobs with some, but not all, of the business subsidy programs. However, there is almost no evidence as to whether these jobs were worth the price the goverments pay for them in terms of lost tax revenues. Finally, considering large regions and the country overall, the business subsidy programs are not administered in a way to provide jobs where they are most needed. As such, in most cases the source of job growth in one locality is job losses in another.

Impact on Equity

If, as Fisher and Peters conclude, business subsidy programs do not redistribute jobs to areas of high unemployment, then it is also unlikely that they have any positive impact on equity. Indeed, if perceived employment gains from business subsidy policies came mainly through poaching jobs from other areas, that leaves only two clear beneficiaries from these policies. The first, of course, are the businesses that receive the subsidies. The second are the purchasers of the government-subsidized bonds. Citizens for Tax Justice reports that 73 percent of the tax benefits from all municipal bonds goes to those earning over $200,000 per year, and there is no reason to assume that the tax benefits for the municipal bonds targeted specifically as Industrial Development Bonds would have a more equitably distributed group of owners.

It should not be surprising that business subsidy programs do not have a positive impact on equity, since, as Fisher and Peters's discussion makes clear, that is not normally a major priority of these programs in the first place. By contrast, "economic growth" has been a major priority, but this term can encompass a wide range of specific meanings. In practice, it has usually meant support for downtown business developments, with the vague anticipation that such support will eventually also yield benefits for the poor and unemployed.

The experience in Cleveland since the early 1980s provides a dramatic case study of how business-subsidy urban development strategies affect social equity.[12] In 1978, Cleveland defaulted on its fiscal obligations, thereby creating a perception that the city was experiencing a severe long-term decline. However, since the late 1980s, Cleveland has been dubbed "The Comeback City" through dozens of positive stories in the news media. The basis for the new perception of Cleveland was the rebuilding of parts of its downtown to attract corporate headquarters, entertainment, and tourism. The first cornerstone of this strategy was the construction of the Gateway Sports Complex. This cost nearly $700 million, and was 75 percent publicly funded. A second major project was the $400 million conversion of the original Cleveland Union terminal into a shopping plaza/hotel complex. The total public subsidy for this project was $200 million. A third major project—including the construction of a fifty-seven-story office tower, a new Marriot hotel, and a historic bank building restoration—received approximately $100 million in tax credits and abatements for the $430 million project. The new Rock and Roll Hall of Fame, most of whose $92 million in construction costs came from publicly held debt, is the fourth recently completed major downtown project. As we write, plans are proceeding to construct a new $250 million, publicly financed football stadium as well.

Despite these high-visibility projects, Cleveland's basic socioeconomic problems show virtually no improvement. Since 1990, the county has suffered a 1.3 percent loss of total jobs while the state increased the number of jobs by 19 percent. The loss of total jobs has meant the total county payroll has dropped by $414 million. From 1970 to 1994, poverty in Cleveland rose substantially from 17 percent to 28 percent. As of 1994, Prof. Norman Krumholz of Cleveland State University places the poverty rate as high as 42 percent. The unemployment rate for African Americans in 1990 was more than 20 percent, the highest of any major city in the United States. The non-employment rate (unemployed, not looking for work, or in jail) of young black men 18–25 hovers near 50 percent.

In 1995, the Cleveland school system, whose operating budget had lost hundreds of millions of dollars through the tax abatements, was put into receivership. By 1997, the Cleveland Teachers' Union and other groups led a petition drive for a referendum to limit further abatements, making Cleveland the first city in the country to vote on such a referendum. The measure initially had widespread support, but ultimately lost by 58 percent to 42 percent after the city's business interests financed an aggressive, big-budget media campaign to defeat it.

Some supporters of Cleveland's downtown development strategy recognize that the city's severe social problems have persisted, but nevertheless defend the subsidies to business. For example, Prof. Paul Gottlieb, associate director of the Center for Regional Economic Issues at Case Western Reserve University, argues that the downtown developments have created jobs for residents in poor neighborhoods, and will continue to do so increasingly as links between downtown and the neighborhoods strengthen.[13] Gottlieb admits that little information exists about wages or other aspects of the jobs for which neighborhood residents commute downtown. Still, he believes that Cleveland's social crisis would only have been worse in the absence of the downtown develop ment projects.

Gottlieb and his colleagues also acknowledge that social equity was never the only goal of the development projects. Their primary purpose was rather to create a "knowledge and leisure" economy, whose amenities would make Cleveland a desirable place for affluent residents and tourists. By this standard, the downtown revival must surely be judged a success. However, the very nature of this success—a glittering downtown amid a worsening social crisis in most neighborhoods—underscores the importance of defining what we mean by "success" in addressing the problems of our cities.

GOVERNMENT OUTSOURCING

Parallel to business subsidy policies, another strategy that municipal governments have adopted increasingly since the late 1980s is to contract out governmental services to private firms, a practice commonly called "outsourcing." The Mercer Group, an Atlanta consulting firm that has closely followed this trend, estimates that between 1987 and 1995, the number of municipalities contracting out particular services increased as follows: Janitorial from 52 to 70 percent, street maintenance from 19 to 38 percent, solid-waste collection from 30 to 50 percent, and data-processing operations from 16 to 31 percent.[14] This trend is parallel to a movement in the private sector in which large corporations eliminate units of their internal operations and contract these out to smaller firms.

What are the reasons for cities to outsource their services? As Prof. Donald Kettl's authoritative 1993 study *Sharing Power* makes clear, the overwhelming one is that private contractors pay lower wages and offer far less generous fringe benefits. Private businesses working under government contracts also aren't bound by civil service protection for employees, which means that they employ more part-time workers and have greater freedom to hire and fire.[15]

The experience in Chicago with outsourcing has been examined carefully by the Chicago Institute on Urban Poverty. They considered the impact of outsourcing on the wage and benefit levels of ten job titles privatized by the city between 1989 and 1995. They found that for each of the entry-level job titles they examined, privatization resulted in dramatic loss of wages and benefits. Losses ranged from a low of 25 percent to a high of 49 percent of workers' annual wages and benefit compensation. Most negatively affected were watchmen (a 49 percent wage and benefit loss), elevator operators (a 46 percent loss), and cashier supervisors (a 44 percent loss). Those experiencing the least severe, though still substantial, losses were parking attendants (a 25 percent loss), security guard supervisors (28 percent loss), and custodial workers (a 31 percent loss). In nearly all cases, the cuts in wages and benefits meant that the annual income of the affected workers fell from a level moderately above to just below that necessary to support a four-person family at the poverty line.[16]

Of course, Chicago has achieved cost savings through such substantial cuts in wages for those performing city services. At the same time, the city also incurs a wide range of new obligations through privatization of services, some of them difficult to control. Direct new costs include the start-up costs of organizing a competitive bidding process to identify the winning contractors; the transition costs in moving from the public to private delivery of the services; the extra contracting costs, such as overruns and renegotiations, that are not included in the initial bids; and the costs of both monitoring the private contractors and providing them with administrative support. Indirect costs also result, in particular an increase in the eligibility for public assistance of the former public-sector workers whose income declines place their families below the poverty line.

Independently of the cost savings through cutting workers' wages and benefits, outsourcing is also often justified on the claim that private businesses are inherently more efficient than the public sector. Efficiency in this sense means that, with a given rate of pay and benefits to workers, a private sector firm will require less labor and materials to provide a fixed amount of city services. When this does happen, then city governments will be able to provide better services to city residents and/or save taxpayers' money through outsourcing. There will, of course, be instances when private firms can perform services more efficiently than the public sector. However, as a general rule, there is no reason why we should expect outsourcing to be more efficient and, in practice, there is no evidence to demonstrate that it has been so on a consistent basis.

Moreover, one need not make heroic claims about the efficiencies of government bureaucracies in order to anticipate potential problems with wholesale municipal outsourcing. Indeed, the problems with outsourcing become most severe precisely if one assumes that government bureaucracies are inefficient and corrupt. When governments are inept or corrupt, then, as Prof. Edward Herman of the Wharton School of Business writes, "contracting out causes competition to assume the form of skillful use of political influence, public relations and even bribery. In addition, profits can be enhanced by carving loopholes in contracts, keeping monitoring weak and capturing regulators."[17]

For municipal governments to bargain effectively with potential contractors, they must at least retain the expertise to be a knowledgeable buyer. But in addition, in cases when private-sector bids are not acceptable, the only way the government can maintain a strong bargaining posture is to be capable of refusing all bids and undertaking the tasks being bid on themselves.

The city of Phoenix, Arizona has been pursuing such an alternative approach—a "public/private competitive process"—since the late 1970s. They have allowed private firms to bid for contracts on virtually all city services, including ambulance service, data entry, refuse collection, senior housing management, and street repair. But the city has maintained its own capabilities in these areas, and has bid against the private firms to retain these services. As a result, neither the city nor the private firms have been able to assume monopolistic control over any city service. In the view of Jim Flanagan and Susan Perkins, the city's auditor and deputy auditor as of 1995, problems of inefficiency and corruption in the delivery of city services emerge as a result of monopolistic control, regardless of whether the city or private firms are the monopolists.[18]

Of course, even with the Phoenix public/private competitive bidding process, the public sector is placed at a disadvantage unless private firms are prevented from making "lowball" bids driven by wage and benefit cuts on the Chicago scale, i.e., of between 25 and 40 percent. Here the need for a living wage minimum could not be more clear. The living wage offers protection to workers in situations where the public sector and private firms bid competitively against one another, such as in Phoenix. Establishing the living wage standard is, in fact, the only way to ensure that such public/private bidding competition will be driven by the relative efficiencies of the public bureaucracies and the private firms, not by a strategy of forcing former civil servants to earn poverty-level wages.

ARE THERE ALTERNATIVES?

Living wage standards are clearly in conflict with the types of business subsidy programs that have dominated municipal policy for nearly two decades. The prevailing business subsidy approach tries to attract firms by offering them the lowest possible costs, while living wage programs prevent firms from paying poverty wages as a means of getting costs down. But as we have seen, the business subsidy approach has not succeeded in alleviating the huge social problems of the cities, since it has failed to produce more jobs or increase social equity. Most evidence suggests this approach has not even succeeded in increasing the number of businesses locating in the targeted areas.

Outsourcing has been the other ascendant municipal policy in the past decade. There is no inherent reason why contracting out of some city services to private firms should conflict with a living wage standard. As we have seen however, the aim of outsourcing is to reduce the costs of city government, and the primary tool for achieving cost savings has been to convert civil service jobs into private-sector jobs with dramatically reduced wages and benefits.

Are there viable alternative municipal policies — that is, policies compatible with a living wage minimum and even supportive of high wages as a component of an urban development program? It is widely held that firms would choose to operate in a city only because of the prospect of minimizing costs through government subsidies and low wages. In fact, however, few businesses make location decisions primarily on the basis of labor costs alone. If they did, they would rarely ever locate in cities, since wages are at least as low in the rural United States, and certainly also in other countries. Similarly, government subsidies are not usually the primary consideration when businesses make location decisions, though firms push for and happily accept subsidies when offered them. When businesses decide to locate in cities, much more important considerations are usually the proximity to suppliers and markets; the quality of the local infrastructure; the quality of the labor force and educational system; and, most broadly, the quality of life in the city, including such factors as the crime rate and range of public amenities. Given these considerations, cities actually have many natural advantages for businesses. The aim of policy should therefore be to nurture these advantages within the framework of a living wage standard for the city's workers.

The economic advantages of cities have recently been described by social scientists in terms of the opportunities cities offer for "agglomeration" or "clustering." These terms refer to the highly productive interrelationships that can form among businesses in densely concentrated urban areas under favorable circumstances. Businesses can benefit from operating within a dense urban cluster in many ways: because their suppliers and markets are close by; because the innovations of any single firm can be more readily diffused throughout the cluster of local firms; because the dense concentration of firms will draw in a larger pool of skilled workers; and because local government spending on infrastructure will be more efficient with the larger number of businesses will benefiting from such expenditures.[19]

For example, Bennett Harrison, Maryellen Kelley, and Jon Gant have shown that the likelihood that manufacturing plants will adopt a new technology (they specifically studied the adoption of computer-programmable automation) is significantly dependent on where the plants are located. The firms that are more likely to adopt new technologies are those that are located in denser urban areas. According to Harrison, Kelley, and Gant, one important reason for this is that managers and engineers of the different firms will know each other as suppliers and buyers and through university and trade association contacts, even if they do not formally share information about their respective production technologies, or are even competitors. Moreover, Harrison, Kelley, and Gant found that the formal linkages and informal avenues of communication among a variety of firms were far more important for how fast the new technology spread throughout an area than whether there were several firms operating in the same line of business.[20]

Understanding the nature of urban economic clusters raises several important points in terms of policy. First, it is not the presence of any single firm that is most likely to generate benefits for a locality, but rather that a cluster of firms develop productive interdependencies. It follows that for such productive interdependencies to occur, the firms that locate within a region should not be there just because they were attracted by a government subsidy, but because the business will benefit from operating within the given cluster. Policy should therefore be aimed at nurturing the firms that have a logical reason to be located where they are; to focus on renewing and upgrading these firms; and to encourage further linkages that build on the basis of existing advantages. Such policies will in turn create an environment in which new businesses will more readily incubate, again, because of existing locational advantages rather than because they are attracted by a subsidy.

Michael Porter of the Harvard Business School has recently argued that even the most economically distressed areas within cities operate on the basis of locational advantages. He in fact finds that there is already considerable business activity occurring in inner-city areas in sectors such as food processing, distribution, printing and publishing, light manufacturing, recycling and remanufacturing, business services for corporations, as well as entertainment and tourist attractions. Porter argues that such businesses as well would gain through an urban strategy that nurtures the benefits of these business clusters.[21]

How should government policies nurture the inherent advantages of cities? One obvious way is to increase spending on public schools, worker training programs, public safety, and an efficient physical infrastructure, as these investments will raise worker productivity and the efficiency of firms. However, investments in these areas can be expensive if they are going to be effective. As we saw with the Cleveland experience, money for improving the public schools was nonexistent after the city's treasury was drained by tax abatements to attract businesses downtown.

However, once investments are made to raise productivity and build on locational advantages, a living wage minimum would be fully consistent with this "high road" development path. Of course, opportunities to raise productivity will make it easier for firms to pay higher wages. But a living wage minimum will itself also encourage both higher productivity and a more vibrant local market.

This is true, first of all, because establishing a living wage minimum forecloses the option of businesses competing through paying poverty wages, forcing them to be competitive by utilizing their workers more productively. As we will discuss further in chapter 5, a living wage minimum also encourages a high-morale workplace in which absenteeism and turnover are lower, and more generally, workers are given incentives to be more productive.

The high-wage, high-productivity route to urban development will also mean that workers will bring more spending power back to their neighborhoods at the end of each day. As Porter and others have shown, businesses are already densely clustered even in poor urban areas. But these businesses would receive a substantial boost when spending power in their neighborhood rises. Neighborhood businesses will also benefit indirectly when local incomes rise. This is because raising workers to wage rates above the poverty line will make them more creditworthy. This will enable residents to acquire loans to start new businesses or to upgrade existing ones.

If the basic thrust of an alternative strategy should be concentrated on improving worker productivity and local infrastructure, thereby strengthening the existing advantages of urban clusters, does it imply that governments should stop awarding subsidies to individual businesses? Michael Porter argues that subsidies are necessary to develop poor urban neighborhoods, but only subsidies that enhance the overall economic environment, such as preparing a site for business by assembling parcels of land, improving infrastructure, performing environmental remediation, and providing better public safety. Beyond this, Porter believes that business should not receive any ongoing operating subsidies because they will distort firms' incentives "with futile attempts to lure businesses that lack an economic reason for locating in inner cities."[22]

But this perspective neglects the ways in which low-cost, carefully targeted subsidies to individual businesses can strengthen the broader urban economy. An example of such an effective subsidy would be a bank loan to an existing small business at below-market rates through the Community Reinvestment Act, the national program inaugurated in 1977 that obligates private banks to provide credit to disadvantaged communities within their regions. Loans under this program would generally have broad community benefits, and meanwhile, would "distort incentives" only to the extent that lending institutions become more favorably disposed to provide credit in poor neighborhoods. Correspondingly, if more credit flowed to poor neighborhoods, perhaps there would be slightly less remaining for other potential borrowers—such as downtown developers, commercial real estate projects, or housing for the affluent. Even this is unlikely to occur, however, since loans through the Community Reinvestment Act, like subsidies in general to high-unemployment areas, are likely to expand total incomes and employment opportunities.

In short, even within an alternative urban policy framework, there will be situations in which business subsidies are appropriate. But unlike the experience with enterprise zones, Industrial Development Bonds and similar programs operating since the early 1980s, such subsidies would need to be made with open eyes as to the goals being sought and the relationship between the expected benefits of the subsidy and its costs. Some guidelines follow.

Subsidies to individual businesses should be awarded only when they are targeted to nurture existing urban clusters as well as benefit any given business.

The costs of a subsidy program relative to its benefits need to be specified clearly. In Cleveland, for example, there is still no clear evidence on how the roughly $1 billion in subsidies for downtown development may have benefited poor neighborhoods. Moreover, neither have any possible benefits been measured against the costs, for example, of the public school system falling into receivership. By contrast, Community Reinvestment Act loans to businesses in poor communities are one important example of a low-cost, highly efficient public subsidy. Even in the short run, there will be no fewer tax dollars for public schools as a result of such loans, nor is there likely to be significantly less credit available for more conventional private projects.

Since we define the most important end of any urban development program as raising the living standard for the majority of city residents, a living wage minimum is an effective policy for ensuring that the types of firms that receive subsidies are the ones that will be contributing the city's development. Thus, the living wage policy adopted in Los Angeles in March 1997 is on the right track in its stipulation that firms must pay the living wage if they receive large subsidies for economic development or job creation.

When subsidies are tied to specific promises by businesses—such as promises to create new jobs and expand their investments—the terms of the subsidy agreement should include what are termed "clawback" provisions. Clawback provisions consist of legally enforceable regulations and contract language that require public funds to be returned, preferably with an interest penalty, if the recipient companies fail to deliver on the stipulated promises. Although quite common in Europe, clawback provisions have only recently been adopted by various state and local governments in the United States, including Ohio, Illinois, Connecticut, and Vermont; New Haven, Connecticut; and Austin, Texas.

4—How Much Do Living Wage Laws Cost and Who Pays for Them?

In this chapter, we consider how much living wage ordinances cost. The primary costs come from the increase in wages and benefits to low-wage workers. But the costs resulting from low-wage workers getting a raise also bring substantial *benefits*, primarily to the low-wage workers and their families, but more broadly as well. We therefore examine the economic impacts of living wage ordinances in terms of their benefits in chapter 5.

As we discussed in chapter 1, living wage proposals have varied fairly widely in the cities that have adopted or considered them. To give a sense of the range of proposals that have been made and and how their impact would vary, we examine here three different types of proposals:

1. The Los Angeles proposal that became law in March 1997.
2. The more limited ordinance that was passed in the City of Milwaukee in November 1995. (This proposal is separate from similar ones passed by Milwaukee County and the Milwaukee School Board. The terms of the county and school board laws are documented in appendix 2.)
3. Citywide minimum wage initiatives, such as were defeated in Denver in the November 1996 election and Houston in January 1997.

In order to make comparisons between the proposals, we will use the Los Angeles economy as the context for estimating the likely impact of the alternative approaches. For each proposal, we ask: a) how many workers are affected and how large will be their increase in wages and benefits? and b) how many firms are affected and what will be the impact of the mandated wage and benefit increases on these firms' cost structures? In addressing this question, we consider the situation for the average firm and for a range of firms that vary by industry and according to the proportion of low-wage workers they employ.

Once we have assembled the relevant evidence on workers and firms, we are then also able to evaluate the likely impact of living wage ordinances on municipalities as well. We are in a position to ask, in other words, whether the living wage cost increases are likely to be transferred onto city budgets, whether affected firms are likely to relocate, and whether negative employment effects will result.

A RANGE OF ORDINANCES

Table 4.1 presents the central features of the proposals in Milwaukee, Los Angeles, and Denver and Houston. The table distinguishes the proposals under two major categories. The first is the wage and benefit terms of each proposal, including the minimum hourly wage rate and any additional provisions for health benefits and paid days off. The other category is the breadth of coverage of each proposal, distinguished by the type and size of contract that firms hold with the relevant municipality. There are three major contract types to consider: service contracts, such as those to provide legal or janitorial services; concessions, which are the arrangements that typically prevail at a municipal airport or a publicly owned sports arena; and subsidies.

Although our three alternative proposals originated in different cities, all of our empirical estimates are taken from the same Los Angeles database, rather than from separate databases for each city. This approach allows us to observe clearly the relative effects of the alternative proposals themselves, independently of differences in economic conditions among the cities in which the proposals originated. For simplicity, we term the three proposals as "Plan X," the Milwaukee ordinance; "Plan Y," the Los Angeles ordinance; and "Plan Z," the defeated Denver-Houston proposal. The three proposals are labeled as such in table 4.1.

The data are from 1995 unless specified otherwise. This means, in particular, that the operative minimum wage in Los Angeles for our estimates is $4.25, which was the national minimum at that time. Neither the state of California nor LA itself had at that time stipulated a minimum wage above the national rate.

Our methodology of working entirely with Los Angeles data does present some possible problems in using these estimates as a benchmark for other cities, since conditions in Los Angeles are distinct from other large cities. Most importantly, Los Angeles has a significantly higher proportion of low-wage workers than other large cities, with nearly 35 percent of LA workers earning below $7.25 per hour as of 1995 and 8.1 percent earning the 1995 minimum hourly wage of $4.25 or less. In other major cities, between 20 and 26 percent earned below $7.25 in 1995 and 3.3 to 4.5 percent earned the minimum wage or less. This factor will mean that any type of living wage proposal would have a more widespread impact in LA than elsewhere.

What are the central features of the three proposals? As shown in table 4.1, Plan X—corresponding to the ordinance which became law in Milwaukee in 1995—stipulates a minimum hourly wage just sufficient to enable one worker to support a family of three at the national poverty line. In dollar terms, the actual wage rate therefore increases whenever the national poverty thresholds also rise in dollar terms due to

Table 4.1

Alternative Living Wage Ordinances

	Milwaukee "Plan X"	Los Angeles "Plan Y"	Denver-Houston "Plan Z"
Terms of ordinance:			
Wage level	Indexed to poverty level for family of three. Currently at $6.43 per hour.	$7.25	$6.50
Health benefits	Not included	$1.25 per hour	Not included
Paid days off	Not included	12 per year	Not included
Coverage:			
Firms covered	Firms holding *service contracts* of more than $5,000 with the city. Professional services exempted.	Firms holding *service contracts* of $25,000 or more; firms with *concession arrangements; firms that receive financial assistance* of $1 million, or $100,000 annually on an ongoing basis for economic	All firms with employees who work within the city limits.

Workers covered	All employees of covered firms.	development; subcontractors of the above firms. All employees who work directly on the contract or subcontract, work at the concession, or spend at least 50% of their time on a subsidized project or at the subsidized site.	All employees who work inside the municipality.
Exemptions	None	Nonprofits, unless CEO pay is more than 8 times that of lowest paid employee.	None

inflation. As we write, that hourly wage rate is $6.43, which we have rounded up to $6.50. There are no additional provisions for health benefits or paid days off. This proposal covers only firms that hold service contracts of over $5,000 with the city, and among the service contracts, exempts firms providing professional services, including legal, engineering, and architectural firms.

Plan Y—corresponding to the ordinance which became law in Los Angeles in March 1997—sets the minimum wage at $7.25. It also includes health benefits of $1.25 per hour for workers without private health insurance and requires 12 paid days off per year for all workers. This proposal covers all firms holding service contracts of over $25,000 per year as well as these firms' subcontractors. Only the employees of the affected firms who work on the specific contract are directly covered by the law (though in later discussions we will also consider how the uncovered workers within affected firms may also receive benefits). This ordinance also covers firms holding concession agreements with the city as well as firms receiving large subsidies for economic development or job creation. The subcontractors of the affected concessionaires and subsidy recipients are also covered by the LA ordinance.

Finally, Plan Z is modeled on those considered but defeated in both Denver and Houston. These were straightforward citywide minimum wage ordinances, with the minimum hourly wage in both cases set at $6.50. These proposals did not have any provisions for health benefits or paid days off. We consider the impact of this one proposal in terms of Los Angeles County rather than, more narrowly, the City of Los Angeles alone. We do this first because it provides us with one scenario whose range exceeds the city limits proper. But most importantly, for Los Angeles and other areas as well, the countywide data on employment, wage rates, and the production of goods and services by firms are much more reliable than those for the city proper.

DATABASE CONSTRUCTION AND METHOD OF ESTIMATION

Estimating the impact of most living wage proposals requires information about the specific firms holding contracts with the municipality in question. In our three alternative scenarios, only Plan Z does not require such information. There are three possible ways to obtain the necessary information. The first is to obtain information directly from all the firms affected by the living wage proposal. The second is to sample a subset of these firms, and, grouping the firms according to the federal government's Standard Industrial Classification (SIC) codes or some other method, estimate results for the full set of firms from the sampled subset. The third is to group the affected firms by SIC codes and, rather than sampling the firms, utilize the government's own SIC-based sample information to estimate the relevant characteristics of the affected firms.

Assuming one could obtain the cooperation of all or a high proportion of the affected firms, receiving direct data from them would probably yield the most reliable results. However, such comprehensive information is difficult to acquire, and even if it could be obtained, it could still be unreliable if the people being sampled had some stake in the outcome of the study. For example, businesspeople opposed to a living wage ordinance could inflate the number of low-wage workers in their firm if they wanted to exaggerate the costs they would incur through such an ordinance.[1] Other than acquiring data from all affected firms, there are merits to both of the other two approaches—relying on either a partial sample of firms or on the government's sampling information. Not least among the advantages of relying on government sampling statistics is that it enables one to construct a database relatively quickly and cheaply and does not require the cooperation of affected businesses.

Our method is an amalgam of the latter two approaches, though it draws most heavily on government figures (details of our approach are presented in appendix 3). First, to the extent possible, we constructed a database including all the firms holding contracts, concession agreements, or subsidies of the relevant types with the City of Los Angeles. We then categorized the firms according to the government's SIC classification system. For the most part, we then derived estimates of the number of low-wage workers, the wage rates of these workers, and the production of goods and services of the affected firms from separate government sources. Finally, for a small but significant subset of firms, we did have access to direct data on their number of employees, wage rates and/or levels of production. We utilized these data in two ways: first by directly incorporating them into our database as appropriate; and, more generally, as a check on the reliability of the figures derived from the government sources.

ESTIMATED COSTS OF ALTERNATIVE LIVING WAGE PROPOSALS

We present estimates beginning with the costs mandated by law, including the mandated wage increases, health benefits, and paid days off. Firms affected by living wage ordinances will also have to devote some of their resources to demonstrating their compliance with the new regulations. City governments, in turn, will have to devote some resources to monitoring and enforcing compliance. We group all mandated wage, benefit, and compliance costs as the "direct costs" of the alternative living wage proposals. We treat the cities' monitoring and enforcement costs separately, in examining the impact of the ordinances on city budgets.

We also consider an indirect cost, the "ripple effect" that will likely occur within the affected firms when only some workers—i.e. the lowest-paid workers—get a raise. For these affected firms, we anticipate many other workers within the same broad pay range will also get raises, even though their raises will not be mandated by the living wage ordinance. Adding direct and indirect effects then enables us to estimate the total costs of the living wage proposals for the affected firms.

DIRECT COSTS

Table 4.2 presents estimates for the number of firms and workers directly affected by the alternative proposals, as well as the wage increases associated with each proposal.

The Impact of outliers

As table 4.2 shows, we have generated two sets of estimates for Plan Y. This is because our research found strong, if not conclusive, evidence that six large firms with a substantial number of low-wage workers fall under the terms of Plan Y as subsidy recipients. The largest of these firms is in the construction industry. The others are in printing and publishing, food processing, trucking and water transportation. If our estimates of the size and employment profile of these

Table 4.2
Direct Wage Costs to Firms Under Alternative Scenarios

	Plan X	Plan Y– Narrow	Plan Y– Broad	Plan Z
Number of firms affected	469	817	999	284,673
Number of workers affected	1,369	3,924	7,626	870,513
Number of FTE (40 hours per week) workers affected	1,133	3,355	6,521	735,583
Number of FTE (40 hours per week) workers affected per firm	2.4	4.1	6.5	2.6
Average hourly wage before ordinance	$5.07	$5.43	$5.43	$4.94
Average hourly wage increase	$1.43 (to $6.50)	$1.82 (to $7.25)	$1.82 (to $7.25)	$1.56 (to $6.50)
Average yearly wage increase (assumes 2,000 hours of work)	$2,860	$3,640	$3,640	$3,120
Wage increase for year, all FTE workers	$3.2 million	$12.2 million	$23.7 million	$2.3 billion

six firms are accurate, it would mean that nearly half of all workers mandated for wage increases through the ordinance would be employed by these firms.

These firms, in short, are what are termed "outliers" within our sample. One set of results for Plan Y thus excludes these outliers (which we will call "Plan Y–Narrow"), and the other includes them ("Plan Y–Broad"). Through this approach we are able to show how much our estimates for Plan Y depend on whether or not we include these outlier firms in our sample. But there is also a broader, more political, issue to raise, which we also want to emphasize by presenting the alternative scenarios for Plan Y. It is probable that large firms that are significantly impacted by living wage ordinances will, one way or another, try to get themselves exempt from having to abide by the new law. Living wage supporters engaged in monitoring such ordinances should therefore be clear on what is at stake when issues of exemption do emerge. We think providing data on the alternative Plan Y scenarios—one including and the other excluding the outlier firms—contributes to understanding on this question.

Estimates for Four Scenarios

Table 4.2 gives our estimates of direct wage costs. We provide two types of estimates for the number of affected workers. In the second row, we show the total number of affected workers, including both full-time (40 hours per week) and part-time workers. In the third row, we then report figures on "Full Time Equivalent" (FTE) workers. This figure has two components. The full-time workers are counted as before. But the part-timers are counted by adding up their total number of weekly hours, and those total hours are then measured in terms of the number of full-time jobs to which these total hours would correspond.

As we see in table 4.2, significant differences exist between the three citywide proposals, Plan X, Plan Y–Narrow and Plan Y–Broad. Not surprisingly, the impact of Plan Z, the countywide minimum wage ordinance, is of a far greater order of magnitude still.

Plan X has the smallest impact. Though it affects 469 firms, only 1,133 FTE workers would receive benefits from the living wage law. As the average hourly wage of the below $6.50 workers is $5.07, this translates into an average yearly wage increase of $2,860, and the total annual increase in wages under this proposal is $3.2 million.

With Plan Y–Narrow, 817 firms are affected, including subcontractors, and 3,355 FTE workers will receive raises. It is notable that the number of workers affected per firm, at 4.1, is much higher than the 2.4 figure for Plan X. Part of this discrepancy is of course due to the higher wage minimum in Plan Y. But in addition, Plan Y includes firms receiving concessions or large subsidies from the city. These concessionaires and subsidy recipients tend to have a far greater concentration of low-wage workers than the contractors, which are the only type of firm covered in Plan X. We will consider this issue in greater depth below. The average yearly wage increase for these 3,355 workers is $3,640, which brings the total direct wage increase in this scenario to $12.2 million.

The figures for Plan Y–Broad, in column three of table 4.2, document in some detail the impact of the six outlier firms. First, the total number of affected firms rises by 182, to a total of 999 firms. This increase occurs because we estimate that overall, the outlier firms have a substantial number of subcontractors. The number of FTE workers receiving raises is now up to 6,521, which brings the total wage increase to $23.7 million, 1.9 times more than Plan Y–Narrow, the scenario that excludes the outliers. In addition, the average number of affected workers per firm is up to 6.5, reflecting again the substantially greater size of these outlier firms.

Plan Z, again, has far wider scope, and we see the results of this in the fourth column of Table 4.2. We estimate that 284,673 firms and 735,583 FTE workers would be affected by such a proposal. To bring all of these low-wage workers in the county up to a $6.50 minimum would entail an average hourly increase of $1.56, which translates into a $3,120 yearly increase. In all, $2.3 billion in higher wages would go to low-wage workers through the Denver-Houston type proposal.

Health Benefits

Of the three proposals under consideration, only Plan Y includes health benefit coverage. It mandates either employer-provided health coverage or an additional $1.25 per hour for low-wage workers to purchase health insurance themselves. The coverage includes two categories of workers: those earning below the living wage minimum, and those earning up to the living wage minimum plus the additional health coverage. Thus, the second category of workers includes those uncovered workers earning between $7.26 and $8.50 an hour, since the wage minimum in Plan Y is $7.25 and the health provision is $1.25.

For both Plans Y-Narrow and Y-Broad, table 4.3 specifies the impact of the health coverage according to the two affected categories of workers. As the table shows, the total additional cost to provide private health insurance for affected low-wage workers is $5.1 million under Plan Y–Narrow and $10.3 million under Plan Y–Broad.

Table 4.3
Cost of Health Benefits
under Plan Y

	Plan Y– Narrow	Plan Y– Broad
Category 1:		
FTE workers earning below $7.25 per hour	3,355	6,521
Below $7.25 workers without health insurance	1,711 (51% of total)	3,326 (51% of total)
Category 2:		
FTE workers earning between $7.25 and $8.50 per hour	1,078	2,553
$7.25–$8.50 workers without health insurance	334 (31% of total)	791 (31% of total)
Category 1 and 2 total	2,045	4,117
Total annual cost of health benefits ($1.25 per hour for 2,000 hours per worker)	$5.1 million	$10.3 million

Paid Days Off

Only Plan Y includes coverage for paid days off, stipu-
lating a total of 12 days. These requirements are for all
workers in affected firms, not just those below the
living wage minimum. The coverage also includes
part-time as well as full-time workers.

Table 4.4 gives our estimates of the costs of the
paid-days-off provisions under Plan Y. Here again, we
have divided the affected workers into two categories,
those now earning below the living wage and those
above the living wage. For all workers earning below
the living wage, including those not engaged in the
city-contracted work, we estimated their paid days off
at the living wage minimum rate of $7.25.[2] We then
took the average wage of those earning above $7.25 —
which was $18.46 — in generating a cost estimate for
their paid days off. As table 4.4 shows, the total costs of
the paid-days-off provisions are substantial, totaling
$8.3 million under Plan Y–Narrow and $25.1 million
for Plan Y–Broad.

Payroll Taxes and Compliance Costs

The final direct costs include business payroll taxes
and the costs of complying with the living wage ordinance. For 1996, we estimate total business payroll
taxes at 12.5 percent in California, including Social
Security and Medicare (7.65 percent total), federal
and state unemployment insurance (4.4 percent total), as well as state disability (0.5 percent) and the
employer training program (0.1 percent). We have
not included workers' compensation insurance in our
calculation, because of the difficulties of constructing
a reliable average figure. The rates vary, for example,
from 0.29 percent for clerical workers to 7.61 percent

Table 4.4
**Cost of Mandated Paid Days Off
under Plan Y**

	Plan Y–Narrow	Plan Y–Broad
Category 1:		
Low wage FTEs affected	2,449	4,760
(73% of workers below $7.25)		
Total cost for paid days off	$1.7 million	$3.3 million
(at $7.25 per hour)		
Category 2:		
High wage FTEs affected	3,703	7,976
(31% of workers at $7.25 or above)		
Total cost of paid days off	$6.6 million	$14.1 million
(at $18.46 per hour)		
Total costs for mandated paid days off	$8.3 million	$17.4 million

for drivers. By excluding workers' compensation, our 12.5 percent figures for overall payroll tax increases should be considered as a slight underestimate.

As for compliance, under Plan Y, affected firms are required to maintain and preserve complete payroll records of their employees. On January 1 and July 1 of each year, the affected firms will be required to file these payroll records with the city clerk. We estimate the equivalent of one full day of an office worker's time preparing each semi-annual filing. More specifically, we allow that this full day will be divided among professional and secretarial staff. As such, we estimate that the average hourly pay rate for this work is $20 per hour, the equivalent of an average annual salary of $40,000 per year. If we add 15 percent of total labor costs for overhead, we get an annual total of $368 per firm for compliance costs. We calculated compliance costs for Plan X using this same formula. However, for Plan Z, there would be no compliance costs beyond those already incurred under federal and state minimum wage requirements.

Total Direct Costs

As we see in Table 4.5, Plan X and Plan Z are roughly equal in their cost impact per firm, which is not surprising since their wage increases are identical. Plan Y–Broad is by far the most expensive scenario on a per-firm basis, at $54,785 per firm, 64 percent more than the per-firm cost of Plan Y–Narrow. Here again we see the substantial impact of including the outlier firms in our calculations.

INDIRECT COSTS: THE "RIPPLE" EFFECT

The only significant indirect cost of implementing a living wage policy is the "ripple effect" that occurs

Table 4-5
Total Direct Costs Under
Alternative Living Wage Scenarios
(in millions of dollars)

	Plan X	Plan Y-Narrow	Plan Y-Broad	Plan Z
Total wage increase	$3.2	$12.2	$23.7	$2,295.0
New health benefits	—	$5.1	$10.3	—
New paid days off	—	$8.3	$17.4	—
Payroll taxes	$0.4	$1.5	$3.0	$286.9
Compliance costs	$0.2	$0.3	$0.4	—
Total direct costs	$3.8	$27.4	$54.7	$2,581.9
Number of firms affected	469	817	999	284,673
Direct costs per firm (in dollars)	$8,044	$33,569	$54,785	$9,070

when some significant group of workers—but not all workers—in an affected firm get the mandated raise. While workers who are in roughly the same pay range don't necessarily make the same wage or receive increases at the same rate, their pay tends to move together over time, generally in response to firms' wage-setting policies and to local labor market conditions.[3]

With respect to the living wage ordinances, the ripple effect refers to those wage increases that employers give to employees *beyond* what is legally mandated. There are three categories of likely recipients of such wage increases: (1) employees who had previously earned more than the minimum wage but less than the living wage, and who will receive wages that put their new wage above the living wage; (2) employees who had previously earned more than the living wage, and who nevertheless receive a raise when the living wage policy becomes law; and (3) for Plan Y only, those employees within the affected contracting firms who are not involved in their firm's city-related work.

Recent research on the ripple effects arising due to increases in the minimum wage has found that the increases tend to diminish fairly rapidly at higher wage rates, which means that wages will become more equal within the affected firms.[4] However, these studies consider the ripple effects arising from increases in a region-wide minimum wage law, the equivalent of our Plan Z. But they cannot provide adequate guidelines for estimating the effects that may arise from our Plans X or Y—those that mandate wage increases only for the workers employed by a small set of affected firms. Plan Y offers a further significant departure from those studied previously because of its mandate that affected employers give raises to only those workers in the firms who are actually working at least some of their time on the city projects. However, to the extent a ripple effect exists at all, it is likely that *all* workers at the same firm within a given pay range will receive the same raise regardless of how much time they spend on city-contracted projects.

The key question in determining the size of the ripple effect in affected firms is how much of an increase in wage equality will occur in the firm after the lowest-paid workers receive their mandated raises. In studying the impact in Texas of the 1991 federal minimum wage increase from $3.80 to $4.25, the labor economists Lawrence Katz of Harvard and Alan Krueger of Princeton found that the ripple effects of the minimum wage rise in fast-food restaurants was relatively weak, in part because the mandated increase itself was small.[5] They argued that the size of the ripple-effect raises should vary directly with the extent of the mandated increases. Thus, the larger increases associated with the living wage proposals should yield a proportionally greater ripple effect.

An earlier study by the Canadian economists Robert Lacroix and Francois Dussault examined the effects of wage agreements in the public sector on those in the private sector in Canada.[6] They found that the wage spillovers outside of a given firm—whose effects are likely comparable to the ripple effect within a given firm—varied significantly. One influence was the skill level of the workers, with lower-skilled workers enjoying a larger ripple effect in their wages than the higher-skilled. Another important factor was whether the private sector firms were producing goods that would have to compete for sales with international firms.

In all three of our plans, the affected workers are almost all lesser-skilled employees, in which case, following the Lacriox and Dussault findings, the ripple effect would tend to be relatively large. In addition, in

Plan X and Plan Y, the affected firms are service contractors, concessionaires, or subsidy recipients, so they would not be producing goods intended for the export market, and this also would tend to strengthen the ripple effect. In Plan Z, the ripple effect would tend to be correspondingly weaker, since the affected firms would include those competing in global markets with international firms. An additional factor is that part of the aim of the proponents of living wage ordinances is to build from the organizing experiences around the living wage campaigns to support changes in wage norms more broadly within a region. So, to the extent these living wage proponents succeed in getting a living wage ordinance passed, we might assume a greater than normal ripple effect would also follow.

In short, there is considerable uncertainty surrounding the extent of this effect. Accordingly, we present two alternative possibilities that enable us to at least grasp the orders of magnitude involved. These calculations, presented in table 4.6, are based on the $7.25 wage minimum associated with Plan Y.

In Case A, we assume that the 55 percent wage increase for the minimum wage worker will be the largest percentage increase enjoyed in the firm. At higher wage rates, the raises descend first to 35 percent, then, by steps, down to 5 percent, as we move up the pay scale. Obviously, the wage range within affected firms will narrow substantially in this situation. As we see in Case A of table 4.6, the difference between the highest and lowest "mean wage" within our range falls from $4.07 ($8.75 - $4.68) to $1.94 ($9.19 - $7.25). However, even after allowing for such a considerable equalization of wages within affected firms, the total amount of wage increases due to the ripple effect in Case A is $10.8 million. This is almost as large as the total mandated wage increase of $12.2 million in Plan Y–Narrow.

Table 4.6
Alternative Wage Ripple Effects Under Plan Y – Narrow

Pre-ordinance wage range	Mean within range	FTE workers	Case A: Workers up to $9.24 receive declining percentage raise		Case B: Workers up to $8.24 receive declining percentage raise	
			New mean wage	Total wage increase (millions)	New mean wage	Total wage increase (millions)
$4.25–5.24	$4.68	1,795	$7.25 +55%	$9.2	$7.25 +55%	$9.2
$5.25–6.24	$5.79	1,402	$7.82 +35%	$5.7	$7.30 +26%	$4.2
$6.25–7.24	$6.77	1,241	$8.46 +25%	$4.2	$7.45 +10%	$1.7
$7.25–8.24	$7.79	1,290	$8.96 +15%	$3.0	$8.18 +5%	$1.0
$8.25–9.24	$8.75	949	$9.19 +5%	$0.8	$8.75 +0%	$0.0
Total wage increase				$23.0 million		$16.1 million
Wage ripple effect = (total wage increase - mandated wage increase of $12.2 million)				$10.8 million		$3.9 million
Midpoint between Case A and Case B					**$7.4 million**	

Case B in table 4.6 assumes a significantly weaker ripple effect, and thus, even greater equalization of wages within firms due to the living wage ordinance. In this case, only workers earning up to $8.24 receive any benefit from the ripple effect, and those in the $7.25–$8.24 tier receive only a 5 percent raise. The total size of the ripple effect in this case is $3.9 million.

Because of the speculative nature of these calculations, perhaps a reasonable way to proceed in establishing orders of magnitude is to take the midpoint between the Case A and Case B estimates. This means we assume a ripple effect in Plan Y–Narrow of approximately $7.4 million, i.e. about 60 percent of the size of the mandated wage increases resulting from the living wage ordinance.

To roughly estimate the ripple effects for the other scenarios, let us then assume that the effects in these cases are proportional to those for Plan Y–Narrow, after controlling for the size of the mandated wage increase. Such controlling for size refers to the fact that when the new wage floor rises only to $6.50, for example, rather than $7.25, fewer workers are affected and there is less room for maneuver in creating new relative wages within the firm. The sizes of the resulting ripple effect for the other three scenarios is then as follows: Plan X, $1.3 million; Plan Y–Broad, $11.9 million; Plan Z, $986 million.

TOTAL COSTS

Table 4.7 summarizes all direct and indirect costs of the alternative living wage scenarios. It also shows the relative weight of each component in total costs. Thus, with Plans X and Z, direct wage increases account for 61 to 62 percent of total costs, $5.3 million for Plan X and $3.7 billion for the much more far-reaching

Table 4.7
Total Costs of Alternative
Living Wage Ordinances
(in millions of dollars)

	Plan X	Plan Y–Narrow	Plan Y–Broad	Plan Z
Direct Costs:				
Mandated wage increase	$3.2	$12.2	$23.7	$2,295.0
percentage of total increase	60.8%	34.1%	34.8%	62.2%
Health benefits	—	$5.1	$10.3	—
percentage of total increase		14.3%	15.1%	
New paid days off	—	$8.3	$17.4	—
percentage of total increase		23.2%	25.5%	
Payroll taxes	$0.4	$1.5	$3.0	$286.9
percentage of total increase	7.6%	4.2%	4.4%	7.8%
Compliance costs	$0.2	$0.3	$0.4	—
percentage of total increase	3.8%	0.8%	0.6%	
Total direct costs	$3.8	$27.4	$54.8	$2,581.9
percentage of total increase	72.2%	76.7%	80.4%	69.9%

Indirect Costs

Ripple effect raises	$1.3	$7.4	$11.9	$986.0
percentage of total increase	24.7%	20.7%	17.4%	26.7%
Payroll taxes on ripple effect	$0.2	$0.9	$1.5	$123.3
percentage of total increase	3.1%	2.6%	2.2%	3.3%
Total Costs	$5.3	$35.7	$68.2	$3,691.2

Plan Z. With Plan Y, direct wage increases account for much less proportionally—about 34 percent of $35.7 million in Plan Y–Narrow, and of $68.2 million in Plan Y–Broad. As we see in the table, this is because of the large costs associated with the health benefits and especially the paid days off in Plan Y.

IMPACT ON FIRMS AND MUNICIPALITIES

Living Wage Costs Relative to Firms' Total Production Costs

We first consider here the costs of the proposals relative to the firms' total spending to produce goods and services.[7] We examine this both for the "average" firm and by grouping the firms according to the proportion of low-wage workers they employ. This perspective enables us to consider the likely impact of the proposals on firms' operations. In particular, we will want to evaluate how strongly firms are likely to be motivated to push for more favorable terms on city contracts due to a living wage ordinance and/or consider relocating out of cities which obligate them to pay living wages.

Table 4.8 presents figures on total production of goods and services for the affected firms and then calculates ratios of new costs associated with the living wage relative to total costs of producing goods and services. Figure 4.1 also shows the ratio of living wage costs/total production of goods and services for the four scenarios. These figures are quite instructive. Given the total production cost figures we have generated, we see that new costs due to the living wage are quite small in proportion to total production costs—they range from 0.5 percent of total production costs in Plan X to a high of 1.8 percent of total production

Table 4.8
Living Wage Costs Relative to Total
Costs to Produce Goods and Services

	Plan X	Plan Y–Narrow	Plan Y–Broad	Plan Z
Total number of firms	469	817	999	284,673
Total living wage costs	$5.3 million	$35.7 million	$68.1 million	$3.7 billion
Total costs to produce goods and services	$1.1 billion	$2.0 billion	$4.4 billion	$412.6 billion
Living wage total costs	0.5%	1.8%	1.5%	0.9%

Figure 4.1
Living Wage Costs Relative to Affected Firms' Production of Goods and Services

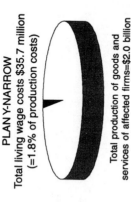

PLAN X
Total living wage costs $5.3 million
(=0.5% of production costs)

Total production of goods and
services of affected firms=$1.1 billion

PLAN Y-NARROW
Total living wage costs $35.7 million
(=1.8% of production costs)

Total production of goods and
services of affected firms=$2.0 billion

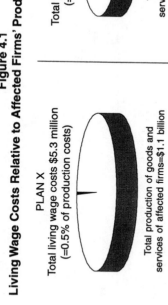

PLAN Y-BROAD
Total living wage costs $68.1 million
(=1.5% of production costs)

Total production of goods and
services of affected firms=$4.4 billion

PLAN Z
Total living wage costs $3.7 billion
(=0.9% of production costs)

Total production of goods and
services of affected firms=$412.6 billion

costs in Plan Y–Narrow. Given the far more extensive coverage of Plan Z, our estimated total production cost figure of about $413 billion is of course much larger than those with the other scenarios. The living wage costs/total production cost ratio, however, at 0.9 percent, represents a mid-range of the four scenarios.

Distinctions Between Firms

Table 4.8 and figure 4.1 give us a sense of the total costs for all affected firms and, correspondingly, for the average affected firm. However, to accurately assess the effect of these proposals, we also need to consider distinctions between firms. In particular, we need to examine differences in the extent to which they employ low-wage workers and therefore in the impact they would experience of a living wage ordinance.

These distinctions among firms will vary, first, according to the different scenarios. Plan X will incorporate the most homogeneous group of firms, since the proposal applies only to contractors. Plan Y includes a more heterogeneous group of firms, because it incorporates subsidy recipients and concessionaires. The inclusion of these types of firms will also tend to bring a higher concentration of low-wage workers per firm. Plan Z will clearly be the most heterogeneous because it incorporates all firms within the county's borders. The figures reported in table 4.2 on the ratio of low-wage workers per affected firm give a sense of the differences among the four scenarios. As we saw there, this ratio ranges widely, between 2.4 workers per firm in Plan X to 6.5 in Plan Y-Broad.

Distribution of Affected Firms by Industry

Table 4.9 provides data by industry on the distribution of affected firms and the proportion of low-wage work-

Table 4.9

Distribution of Affected Firms and Proportion of Low-Wage Workers by Industry Under Plan Y – Narrow (includes 10 most Heavily-Represented Industries)

Industries with highest proportion of affected firms:

Industry Type	Percentage of affected firms	Number of low-wage workers per firm	Characteristic low-wage job
Engineering, accounting, research and management	35.4%	1.2	Receptionist, accounting clerk, data entry
Business services	13.0%	6.9	Janitor clerk, security guard
Amusement and recreation services	5.1%	12.0	Cashier
Eating and drinking places	4.9%	43.4	Dishwasher, waitstaff, bartender
Legal services	3.5%	0.6	File clerk
Social services	2.9%	5.8	Receptionist
Wholesale trade—durable goods	2.4%	1.8	Receptionist, inventory clerk
Motion pictures	2.4%	3.6	Receptionist, security guard
Automotive repair, services and parking	2.1%	5.1	Parking lot attendant
Water transportation	2.0%	0.0	N/A

Industries with highest proportion of low-wage workers:

Industry Type	Proportion of low-wage workers per firm	Percent of affected firms	Characteristic low-wage job
Hotels and other lodging	77.1%	0.3%	Housecleaning, kitchen staff
Eating and drinking places	74.8%	4.9%	Dishwasher, waitstaff, bartender
Agricultural services	71.5%	1.4%	Brush clearance, landscaping
Personal services	66.3%	0.6%	Laundry workers, child care workers
Apparel and accessories stores	66.1%	0.1%	Salesperson, cashier
Miscellaneous manufacturing	60.1%	0.1%	Press operator
Food and kindred products	58.4%	0.3%	Production workers
General merchandise stores	53.1%	0.5%	Cashiers
Home furniture, furnishings, and equipment stores	50.5%	1.0%	Salesperson, cashier
Chemicals and allied products	49.0%	0.1%	Industrial clean-up

ers under Plan Y–Narrow. The upper panel shows the ten industries with the highest proportion of affected firms. As we see, the "Engineering, Accounting, Research and Management" industry is at the top of the list with a full 35 percent of all affected firms. At the same time, these firms have only 1.2 low wage workers per firm. Moving down the list, we see that most of the industries with a high concentration of city contracts also have low proportions of low-wage workers. Such firms should be able to readily absorb the costs of a living wage ordinance.

The lower panel then ranks industries according to their proportion of low-wage workers. These are firms for which a living wage would have a significant impact. For example, in the "Hotels and other lodging" industry, 77.1 percent of the workers would be eligible for a raise under the living wage ordinance. Note here however that virtually all the industries in the lower panel have low proportions of affected firms. For example, only one listed industry in the lower panel, "Eating and Drinking Places" is also on the upper panel listing the industries with high proportions of affected firms. These figures suggest that, for the most part, the impact of the Los Angeles living wage ordinance will be spread thinly among a large number of firms and industries, but that in a few cases, the impact will be substantial.

Distribution of Affected Firms by Living Wage Costs Relative to Total Costs

A still more focused way of grouping the affected firms is to examine them according to their living wage costs relative to the total costs to produce goods and services. Such figures are reported in table 4.10 and are also portrayed in figure 4.2. As the table shows, 662 firms, or 86 percent of the total under Plan

Table 4.10

The Impact of Wage Increases Across the Range
of Affected Firms Under Plan Y–Narrow

Wages of affected workers as a percentage of total firm production costs	Number of firms in category	Percentage of firms in category	Number of workers in category	Percentage of workers in category	Average low-wage costs/total production costs	Average wage increase/ total production costs
0–9%	662	86.0%	1,797	46.0%	3.5%	0.8%
10–19%	56	7.3%	603	15.4%	11.7%	2.4%
20–39%	46	6.0%	667	17.1%	28.0%	11.0%
40–59	—	—	—	—	—	—
60–79%	—	—	—	—	—	—
80–100%	6	0.8%	839	21.5%	85.0%	28.9%

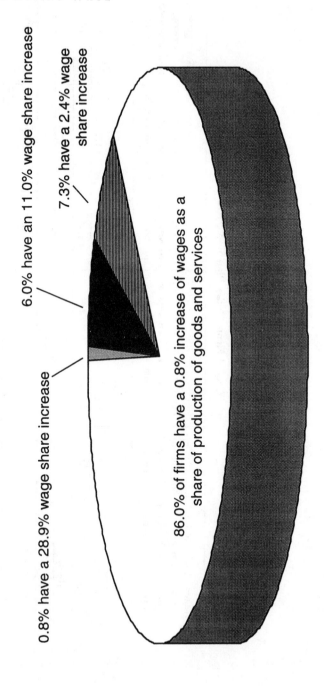

Figure 4.2
Wage Increases as a Share of Total Production of Goods and Services
Across Firms Under Plan Y-Narrow

0.8% have a 28.9% wage share increase

6.0% have an 11.0% wage share increase

7.3% have a 2.4% wage share increase

86.0% of firms have a 0.8% increase of wages as a share of production of goods and services

Y–Narrow—the overwhelming majority of affected firms—have average low-wage costs of 3.5 percent of their total production costs. For these firms, the mandated living wage increases will mean that production costs rise by only 0.8 percent, everything else being equal. Firms in this category should have little difficulty absorbing the extra cost increases due to the living wage ordinance. We may consider these as "low-impact" firms. It is also reasonable to consider among the low-impact firms those for which low-wage costs average 11.7 percent of total production costs, so that the living wage increases would raise production costs by 2.4 percent.

Considering the rest of the firms, 46 (6 percent) will experience cost increases averaging 11 percent, and 6 firms (0.8 percent) will face a cost increase of 28.9 percent due to the living wage.[8] All of these firms—both in the 11.0 and the 28.9 percent cost-increase range can be considered in the "high impact" category. Special consideration clearly must be given to these firms in determining how best to distribute the costs of a living wage increase.

LIVING WAGE ORDINANCES AND MUNICIPAL ECONOMIES

Our estimates of total costs relative to production of goods and services provide the background for considering the impact of these ordinances on the affected municipalities. We must begin here by again acknowledging the difference between Plans X and Y—in which only firms enjoying some type of contractual arrangement with the city fall under the terms of the living wage ordinance—with Plan Z, which applies to all firms within the municipality. We will focus our attention on the narrower Plans X and Y, because little attention has as yet been devoted to analyzing such cases. We then turn briefly to Plan Z, which closely resembles the extensively studied experiences with state minimum wage laws.

Plans X and Y: The Situation for Low-Impact Firms

As we have seen, the total increase in direct and indirect costs for Plan Y–Broad is $68 million. This amounts to 2.1 percent of the $3.3 billion budget of the City of Los Angeles for 1995. A living wage ordinance would therefore represent a substantial, though far from overwhelming, increase in the city's budget if the city were forced on its own to absorb all these new costs. The burden would be roughly equivalent for Milwaukee or other major cities, again, assuming the city would be forced to shoulder all these additional costs on their own. However, we have seen that, on average, the $68 million in living wage–related costs from Plan Y–Broad amounts to only 1.5 percent of total production costs for the affected firms. The average living wage costs/total production cost ratios is slightly higher in Plan Y–Narrow, at 1.8 percent, but is substantially lower in the other two scenarios, falling to 0.5 percent in Plan X. Given these low living wage cost/total production cost ratios for the affected firms, these firms can themselves absorb the bulk of the living wage cost increases. *City governments, in other words, should not have to absorb most of these costs.*

We can see this by considering both the competitive strategies and the organizational structures of the affected firms. The fact that the living wage ordinances will inevitably be phased in over time will further lighten the burden for the affected firms in absorbing the living wage costs themselves. Of course, even for the large majority of firms for which the living wage cost/total production cost ratio is below 1 percent, the affected firms would want to pass on these additional costs through better contract terms with the city. *But the city need not accept these additional costs.*

Competition. We assume that firms are bidding on municipal contracts in a competitive environment. This means that contract holders cannot be assured of getting their contracts renewed, because at least one serious competitor will also bid on a given contract. Studies of municipal contract bidding, such as John Rehfuss's 1989 book *Contracting Out in Government,* make clear that this is the most appropriate assumption from which to begin, even after allowing for extensive lobbying, political jockeying, and corruption in bidding for municipal contracts.[9]

Within such a competitive environment, an increase in costs of roughly 1 percent need not push up contract terms. This is because most firms contracting with cities are eager to maintain their association with the city and would be unlikely to risk relinquishing it to a competitor on the basis of negligible cost increases. This is especially the case if we again recognize that firms make heavy up-front expenditures on lobbying, legal fees, and bribery to win contracts and that, through negotiations conducted in such an environment, contract terms are regularly padded.

Profitability. We have generated a rough estimate for average profitability for the affected firms. Measured as a share of total production of goods and services, we estimated that average profits range between 19 percent for contractors, 13 percent for concessionaires, and 11 percent for subsidy recipients. Thus, even if we assume generously that all firm profits are generated through their city contracts, the profit share would still be 18 percent for contractors, 12 percent for concessionaires, and 10 percent for subsidy recipients.[10]

Productivity. On average, the firms' productivity will be growing as the living wage is implemented. Even if the firms' productivity rises by only 1 percent—i.e., at a rate approximately equal to the average productivity growth rate for nonfarm businesses in the United States for 1990–95—that would mean that productivity growth would itself fully compensate the firms for the increased low-wage labor costs. Of course, redistribution would still occur within the firm, in that one year's worth of productivity gains would be channeled toward the firms' lower-wage workers. But after the one-year adjustment, the distribution of wages and profits within the affected firms could remain constant, while low-wage workers would have received their increases even while income from city contracts did not rise at all.[11]

Overall then, considering the competitive environment, as well as the profitability and rate of productivity growth for the average firm, one can see how the increased costs due to the living wage could be readily absorbed by the low-impact firms. This point is fully consistent with the evidence we reviewed in chapter 2 with both the Baltimore living wage and Davis-Bacon prevailing wage laws. In the case of Baltimore, the researchers Mark Weisbrot and Michelle Sforza-Roderick found that, after implementing its living wage ordinance, winning bids on city contracts increased by less than 0.25 percent before adjusting for inflation, and, after adjusting for inflation, *fell* by 2.4 percent relative to their pre–living wage figures. From interviews with contractors in Baltimore, Weisbrot and Sforza-Roderick found that while some contractors did take account of the mandated wage increases in their bids, other factors overwhelmed the impact of these cost increases.[12] With the Davis-Bacon laws in the construction industry, the pattern is that the wage standards have reduced the proportion of irresponsible "lowball" bids and correspondingly increased competition among firms able to compete on the basis of efficiency and quality of work.

The Situation for High-Impact Firms.

As we have seen, under Plan Y–Narrow, roughly 7 percent of firms fall in the high-impact range, with cost increases of 10 percent or greater. That proportion would be slightly lower in Plan Y–Broad, and probably lower still in Plan X and Plan Z. The cost increases experienced by the high-impact firms clearly must be treated differently from those for low-impact firms. But it still does not follow that living wage cost increases must be borne entirely by city budgets.

As a first countervailing factor, the high-impact firms should also experience faster than average productivity growth. Two factors that will likely raise productivity after workers receive their living wage increases are increased effort due to higher morale and lower rates of turnover. In chapter 5, we discuss these factors in some detail as benefits to firms of the living wage. For now though, we just note that the research that has examined these effects ranges widely in trying to quantify their impact. And while we therefore should expect some positive impact, it is difficult to provide even a reliable range as to how substantial that impact will be.

In any case, it is reasonable to allow that productivity gains due to the living wage increases would not fully compensate for the cost increases of 10 percent or greater that high-impact firms would experience. Municipal governments will therefore have to expect some pass-throughs of living wage costs by these firms. Nevertheless, this can still be done without imposing any significant costs on the city's budget or any loss of city services. Three considerations are crucial:

A large percentage of the high-impact firms are concessionaires. These firms operate on city property but sell goods and services to the public. Most of their cost increases can be passed on through higher prices. At the same time, these price increases will be constrained because the firms are operating in a competitive consumer market, selling goods with low unit costs. Market competition in such situations should therefore push concessionaires to absorb part of their living wage cost increases through productivity gains and a redistribution of wages and profits within the firm.

For the relatively small percentage of high-impact firms that are city contractors and subsidy recipients, the city should expect that new contracts will provide better terms for the firms. But even allowing for this in perhaps 5 to 6 percent of all contracts, the overall impact on the city budget can be minimized through small reductions in contract terms among the 90 to 95 percent of low-impact firms. In this case, such small reductions in contract terms for the low-impact firms would mean, at worst, that the city's reliance on service contractors would grow slightly less rapidly over the years in which the living wage increases are implemented. For example, relative to the growth of its budget, the city would reduce slightly the total amount of its contracts to private engineering, accounting, and management consulting firms—the most heavily concentrated type of firm holding city contracts—while the living wage ordinance is being phased in.

Because both a Plan X and Plan Y living wage ordinance affect only firms doing business with the city government, in practice the ordinance will most likely be phased in gradually, rather than imposed abruptly.

This is because the impact of the ordinance on any given affected firm will be felt only when existing contracts terminate and new ones are put out for bid. In Los Angeles, service contracts with the city normally run for three years, while concessions generally run between five and ten years. In Milwaukee, some service contracts can be as brief as two to three months, but many contracts also run as long as three years. On top of this, cities may choose to formalize the process of phasing in their ordinance through raising the mnimum wage in a series of steps. As we saw in chapter 2, this was done in Baltimore, where the living wage was set at $6.10 for 1995, then raised to $6.60 in July 1996. Beyond that, the ordinance stipulates that the wage will increase annually, upon approval of the Board of Estimates, until it equals the amount required to raise a family of four above the poverty line.

City Monitoring Costs

In Los Angeles, the city has hired five "management analysts" to be compliance monitors for its living wage ordinance. If each of these monitors is paid at the high end of the city's management analyst pay scale ($44,400 in 1996), that would bring direct monitoring costs to $222,000. Adding 15 percent for overhead costs such as secretarial support, rent, and office expenses brings the total to $255,000. This is certainly not an overwhelming burden within a 1996 budget of $3.4 billion. Moreover, other cities with living wage ordinances have adopted roughly equivalent staffing levels.

The more significant question, which we raised in chapter 1, is whether the responsible government officials will actually fulfill their responsibilities in enforcing the ordinances that have passed. The early experience, especially in cities such as New York and

Los Angeles, where the mayors opposed the measures that passed, has been that city officials subsequently sought to provide exemptions from the law for as many businesses as possible and to minimize official enforcement efforts. Living wage proponents clearly cannot expect the government monitors to adequately enforce the law without being pressured to do so. Fortunately, firms which comply with the law will be natural allies of living wage advocates in insisting on proper enforcement, especially in situations where complying firms lose government contracts to violators.

The Relocation Effect Under Plan Z

Under either Plans X or Y, no incentive exists for firms to relocate. This is because the ordinance will affect firms that have contracts with the city, regardless of where they are located. But under Plan Z, falling under the terms of the ordinance does depend on whether the firm is located within the municipal boundaries, or, if it is outside the municipality, whether the firm's employees actually do their work within the city's limits.

Raising the minimum wage for firms within a given municipality will therefore create an incentive for firms to move to neighboring municipalities which have lower minimum wage requirements. However, the force of this effect will depend, first, on how large the firms' newly mandated wage costs are relative to other considerations. With low impact firms, the incentives to relocate will be minimal under all circumstances.

But even with a large proportion of high-impact firms, the costs of relocation will exceed the expected benefits. "Eating and drinking establishments," for example, are likely tied to their specific locations. Employees at such firms alone constitute 17 percent of all the affected workers in Plan Z. Many other firm types with a high proportion of low-wage workers—such as general merchandise stores and tourist-based businesses such as hotels—are also tied to their existing locations. "Business service" firms—such as those providing janitorial services—are not tied to their existing locations. However, if their employees were working within the boundaries of the municipality, they would still fall under the terms of the living wage ordinance. These firms as well would thus have little incentive to relocate.

The types of firms for which the benefits of relocation would exceed costs would be high-impact firms whose business is in no way location-specific. In table 4.11 we have listed the types of firms that fall under this category, their proportion of total affected businesses, and their proportion of total affected workers. Not surprisingly, these are all manufacturing firms.

Table 4.11 also reports our estimates of the amount of business taxes paid by these firms, in order to provide a rough measure of the direct losses that the municipality would experience if these firms were to locate outside its limits. As we see, this figure would amount to about $34 million, assuming that all of the firms in these industries did relocate. This is a significant number, of course, but it is only 1 percent of the $3.2 billion in direct and indirect wage increases that workers would enjoy under Plan Z.

This figure may somewhat underestimate the total costs to the city of relocation, since we were not able to generate a reliable figure for decline in the city's property tax revenues, and the corresponding decline in property values that would result from these firms abandoning their city locations. We have also not estimated the impact of the departure of these firms on

Table 4.11

High-Impact Industries Likely to Relocate under Plan Z

2-digit SIC	Industry name	Total LA County establishments	Percent of workers earning less than $6.50	Estimated annual business tax per firm	Estimated total business taxes for industry
23	*Apparel and other textiles*	5,353	70.4%	$1.554	$8,318,562
31	*Leather and leather products*	110	42.9%	$2,498	$274,780
22	*Textile mill products*	340	40.0%	$4,609	$1,567,060
24	*Lumber and wood products*	564	36.7%	$1,524	$859,536
39	*Miscellaneous manufacturing*	851	35.1%	$2,800	$2,382,800
30	*Rubber and misc. plastics products*	725	25.0%	$5,974	$4,331,150
25	*Furniture and fixtures*	801	23.4%	$3,450	$2,763,450
20	*Food and kindred products*	758	20.1%	$17,728	$13,437,824

Total Business Tax: $33,935,162

the businesses of their neighboring firms. On the other hand, it is unlikely that all of the affected firms would be motivated to leave the city, especially since firms do incur costs associated with moving. They may also lose the benefits that we described in chapter 3 of operating within a cluster of city-based firms, all of which achieve productivity gains through their mutual association.

We have assumed no impact due to loss of employment within the city limits. This is because the workers employed by these firms would not relocate their private residences. Therefore the expenditures and sales tax they bring to the city would not be affected by their employers' relocation. Of course, both expenditures and sales taxes within the city would fall if the firms relocated to further distances, forcing workers to relocate their residences. But there is nothing in Plan Z that would encourage firms to undertake such moves.

Employment Effects

Two interactive factors that we have considered may produce negative employment effects. The higher wages and better benefits for low-wage workers creates an incentive for employers to hire fewer such workers. In addition, if workers respond to their better compensation by increasing their productivity, fewer workers are then needed to perform any given task.

As we noted in chapter 2, it is important to distinguish between *employment loss* and changes in the *unemployment rate*. When we say that no employment loss should occur, that means that no firm should have to lay off workers to meet the terms of the ordinance. Increases in the unemployment rate—the proportion of workers actively seeking jobs who are unable to obtain them—can occur for a variety of reasons, including that more low-income people might begin seeking jobs once the opportunity of earning a substantially higher wage presents itself. Increases in the unemployment rate that occur for this reason should not be regarded as a negative consequence of the ordinance.

We saw in chapter 2 that increases in minimum wages even in the range of 20 percent will not necessarily cause employment losses. Moreover, we saw there was no statistical association between movements in the real value of the minimum wage and the *unemployment rate*, in considering this relationship both for the entire labor market and that for teenagers only. This suggests that other factors in the economy, in particular the level of overall demand for goods and services—that workers would be employed to provide—is far more important than the minimum wage in determining the level of employment and unemployment in the economy. This does not mean that, everything else equal, increases in minimum wages may not encourage employers to consider replacing minimum wage workers with higher-skilled workers or that there are no bounds as to how high the minimum wage could rise without producing negative employment effects. What the evidence rather shows is that within the range at which minimum wage increases have occurred, the factors which might reduce jobs for low-wage workers are dominated by other factors affecting employment.

However, this may not be the situation for Plan Y, in which the raise to $7.25 would be about 34 percent above the $5.43 average wage for workers affected by this ordinance. Moreover, affected workers who do not have health coverage or paid days off would be receiving these as well under Plan Y. Such gains in total compensation are clearly beyond the experiences we have observed with national or statewide minimum wage increases.

We do not know, therefore, whether a Plan Y living wage ordinance would cause employment losses among the affected firms. However, as we have seen, for the types of firms that would be affected by Plan Y, in most cases, the labor cost increases are small relative to firms' total production of goods and services. Thus, for most of these low-impact firms, employment decisions will depend far more on the level of demand for the goods and services they produce than the living wage cost increases. As for the majority of high-impact firms, we have shown how adjustments in these firms' pricing strategies and contract terms with the relevant municipalities can absorb these costs without creating major disruptions in these firms' operations. Demand for workers by these firms should correspondingly remain fairly stable.

Given all this, it is still possible, especially under Plan Y, that affected firms may choose to reduce their workforce or replace their existing low-wage workers with workers that they feel are more deserving of the higher wages. But, as we discuss in chapter 5, even such actions per se by affected firms do not cause employment loss if the workers laid off by the affected firms are able to find jobs elsewhere. Whether they would find other jobs, in turn, depends far more on overall economic conditions in the municipality and region than the impact of a Plan Y–type municipal living wage ordinance. If for no other reason then, even Plan Y should have little overall employment impact because it would affect so small a proportion of the total number of firms and workers in a municipality. But what if Plan Y were more broad-based; for example, what if the terms of Plan Y applied to an entire county, as in the case of Plan Z, or even more broadly, to a state or the country as a whole? We would have to take seriously the possibility that, if everything else about the economy stayed the same, such a large increase in total compensation could create widespread employment losses. This is why, in chapter 6, we take up precisely the question: under what conditions would it be feasible for a $7.25 or higher national minimum wage to be consistent with a full-employment economy?

CONCLUSION

All of the alternative living wage ordinances will produce costs that are substantial in terms of their absolute numbers. $3.5 billion in wage increases under Plan Z is a lot of money. So, for that matter, is the $4.8 million in new wage costs in Plan X, the most narrow of the plans.

However, as we have seen, these costs are not large relative to the total production of goods and services by the firms that will be affected by the various ordinances. In fact, the wage and benefit increases for most firms due to the living wage requirements will be less than 1 percent of these firms' total spending to produce goods and services. As such, we have shown that the living wage ordinances will likely have negligible effects on the behavior of most affected firms. They are also likely to have negligible effects on the budgets of municipal governments, as long as the governments do not concede that the cost increases generated by the ordinances should, as a matter of course, be absorbed by themselves.

A small number of firms that employ a high concentration of low-wage workers will face a substantial cost increase in meeting the living wage requirements. In both Plans X and Y, where the ordinances apply only to firms conducting business with the city government, the city should expect to absorb some of these new costs. But even here, the budgetary impact of any pass-throughs can be limited after allowing that: (1) many of the firms are concessionaires, who also have the option of raising prices; (2) a Plan X or Plan Y–type ordinance will necessarily be phased in over several years; and (3) relative to the growth of its overall budget, the city can reduce slightly its reliance on service contractors such as engineering, management consulting, and accounting firms in the years the living wage ordinance is phased in, and such reductions can be spread widely enough through the city budget so the effect would not be noticeable for city residents. This combination of factors—the low impact of the ordinance on most affected firms, and the ability to spread the costs faced by the small number of high-impact firms—helps explain why the Baltimore ordinance, which has been in place since 1995, has thus far had essentially no impact on city contract patterns or the city's budget.

Perhaps the largest single cost to municipalities would be tax losses under Plan Z, due to relocations out of the boundaries of the municipality. But even here the likely costs are small relative to the wage gains to workers and the total revenue base of municipalities.

How significant are all these costs? We can't know this until we consider them relative to the benefits that accrue to workers and their families, as well as the broader community. We thus now turn to assessing these benefits.

5—Who Benefits From the Living Wage?

The primary beneficiaries of living wage ordinances are the affected workers and their families, whose living standards will rise when such ordinances become law. But there are other beneficiaries as well. These include the various branches of the government, which benefit when the subsidies they pay to working poor families decline. It also includes, as we have already briefly mentioned, the affected firms, which benefit through the increase in morale that a living wage workplace encourages. Finally, the communities in which the affected workers live will gain modestly when the workers bring home increased spending power into their communities.

HOW MUCH WILL LIVING STANDARDS RISE FOR WORKERS AND THEIR FAMILIES?

Living wage ordinances are designed not just to raise the living standard of individual workers, but also to allow low-wage workers to earn enough to raise a family decently. We therefore consider here the impact on a worker and her/his family of receiving the wage and benefit gains through a living wage ordinance. To do this, we examine the case for a family of four under Plan Y (based on the Los Angeles ordinance) and Plan Z (based on the 1996/97 proposals defeated in Denver and Houston). Because the $6.50 living wage minimum in Plan Z is identical to that in Plan X (based on the Milwaukee ordinance), the impact for the individual worker under Plan X will replicate that in Plan Z, and therefore need not be examined separately.[1]

Drawing from our Plan Y data, we assume that the one family member with a job works full-time (2,000 hours/year), earning $5.43 an hour and with no private health benefits before passage of the living wage ordinance. After passage of the ordinance, the worker would earn $7.25 an hour in wages and $1.25 in health benefits. To calculate the net benefits of Plan Y, we measure gains in family income, but also changes in tax obligations and government subsidies. We then perform a comparable exercise under the stipulations of Plan Z. The one family member with a job earns the sample average of $4.94 an hour, and receives a raise to $6.50 an hour. Otherwise, in this case, the living wage ordinance will not bring any additional benefits. But the raise increase alone will also bring changes in tax obligations and subsidies, which we will present. All of these effects are shown in tables and figures 5.1 (Plan Y) and 5.2 (Plan Z). The detailed calculations underlying the figures discussed here are presented in appendix 4.

Changes in Family Income and Subsidies Under Plan Y

As we see in table 5.1, the rise in hourly wages from $5.43 to $7.25 means a $3,640 increase in pretax income for the low-wage family, from $10,860 to $14,500. However, this wage increase then means that the family pays more in federal and state taxes. The change in after-tax earned income is $2,871, from $9,997 to $12,868. With the inclusion of private health insurance, the after-tax gain from the living wage ordinance comes to $5,371.

Table 5.1
Family Benefits under Plan Y
Based on Los Angeles Ordinance
(2,000 hours of work/year)

	Wage = $5.43/hour	Wage = $7.25/hour
1) Gross annual income	$10,860	$14,500
2) Federal income tax	$0	$521
3) FICA tax	$776	$995
4) California state income tax	$0	$0
5) State disability insurance	$87	$116
6) After-tax earned income (=row 1 - (rows 2+3+4+5)	$9,997	$12,868
7) Private health coverage	$0	$2,500
8) After-tax earned income plus private health coverage (= rows 6 + 7)	$9,997	$15,368
9) Earned income tax credit	$3,110	$2,456
10) Food stamps	$3,528	$2,556
11) Disposable income (= rows 6 + 9 + 10)	$16,635	$17,880
12) MediCal coverage	$2,160	$910
13) LA County indigent health coverage	$994	$0
14) Disposable income plus non-indigent health care (= rows 7 + 11 + 12)	$18,795	$21,290
15) Percentage of disposable income from wages (= rows 6/row 11)	60.1%	72.0%
16) Total government subsidy (= rows 9 + 10 + 12 + 13)	$9,792	$5,922

We then calculate changes in after-tax income after accounting for all government benefit sources, including publicly funded health care. As table 5.1 shows, at $5.43, the family's disposable income, after accounting for the earned income tax credit (the "EITC" is the federal program that provides a cash payment to working families whose incomes fall below a certain level) and food stamps, is $16,635, and their disposable income plus health coverage is $18,795. Under the living wage ordinance, the family's disposable income is $17,880 and their income plus health coverage comes to $21,290. As we show in the last two rows of the table, the family's total government subsidy has fallen from $9,792 to $5,922. Correspondingly, the percentage of their disposable income earned from wages has risen from 60.0 percent to 72.0 percent. In other words, the family has become substantially more self-sufficient, i.e., less reliant on government support to maintain themselves.

Figure 5.1 summarizes these changes by showing percentage gains in various measures. First, as we see, the living wage ordinance would bring the family a 33.5 percent gain in pretax earned income. But the family will now pay more in taxes and receive less through the earned income tax credit and food stamps. Their support through MediCal and the LA County indigent health care system also declines. As one overall measure of their change in well-being, figure 5.1 shows the family's increase in disposable income and non-indigent health care, this amount increasing by 13.3 percent. Beyond this, the figure reports two other measures of the family's well-being: the one member of the family now enjoys 4.8 percent more free time due to the paid-days-off provision of the living wage ordinance; and the family's reliance on government subsidies has fallen by 39.5 percent.

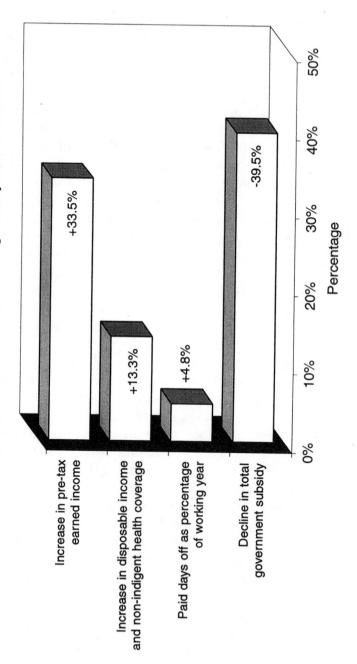

Figure 5.1
Plan Y: Changes in Income and Subsidies for Low-Wage Family After Ordinance

Considering all these post–living wage adjustments, the low-income family benefits in five direct ways: their earned incomes increase; their spending power increases; they have access to better health care; they enjoy the paid days off of the family's working member; and they rely less on government subsidies.

In addition to these, two other considerations must be recognized in evaluating the overall impact of this living wage ordinance on the low-income family. The first is that the family will have significantly greater access to bank loans and other forms of credit, which can be used to purchase a home or automobile or to finance higher education. This is because lending institutions measure a borrower's creditworthiness on the basis of their earning power—which has risen by 33.5 percent. Lending institutions would tend to discount in-kind benefits from the government, such as food stamps or health care, and even cash benefits such as the earned income tax credit in measuring whether a loan applicant will be creditworthy.[2]

In addition, there is the issue of dignity. The United States has spent decades debating its welfare system, culminating with the passage of the 1996 law requiring welfare recipients to work. Regardless of the merits of this particular law, there is one point on which all parties to the welfare debate agree: that earning a dollar of income has dramatically different effects on a person's self-image and attitude toward life and work than being given a dollar of government subsidies. As we have seen, passage of the Plan Y living wage ordinance—the actual ordinance in place in Los Angeles—will mean that the low-income family's reliance on government subsidies will fall by a substantial 39.5 percent.

Changes in Family Incomes and Subsidies Under Plan Z

Table 5.2 and figure 5.2 present results for Plan Z comparable to those we have just reviewed for Plan Y. Of course, Plan Z will provide significantly smaller increases in well-being for the individual families, since the wage increase is only to $6.50 an hour, and no additional benefits or paid days off are included. (At the same time, with Plan Z, unlike Plan X, the gains from the living wage would be spread over far more families than with Plan Y.)

We again present results for a family of four with one wage-earner and two children. In table 5.2, we see that the family's pretax income would rise from $9,880 to $13,000 and that after-tax earned income rises from $9,095 to $11,380. After including the earned income tax credit and food stamps, the family's disposable income has risen from $15,973 to $17,152. These changes are all summarized in figure 5.2. It shows that pretax income rises by 31.6 percent, while disposable income rises by much smaller, but still significant 7.4 percent. Meanwhile, the family's reliance on non–health related subsidies has fallen by 16.1 percent.

As with Plan Y, the family will also benefit indirectly through the living wage, since they become more creditworthy because of the 25.9 percent gain in after-tax earned income. They also have become substantially less dependent on government subsidies.

How Representative Is Our Low-Wage Family?

The figures we have just reviewed on living wage impacts for families depend on the size and behavior of the low-wage family. But have we reasonably described the family circumstances of low-wage workers? And to

Table 5.2
Family Benefits Under Plan Z
Based on 1996/97 Denver-Houston Proposals
(2,000 hours of work/year)

	Wage = $4.94/hour	Wage = $6.50/hour
1) Gross annual income	$9,880	$13,000
2) Federal income tax	$0	$521
3) FICA tax	$756	$995
4) California state income tax	$0	$0
5) State diability insurance	$79	$104
6) After-tax earned income (= row 1 - (rows 2+3+4+5)	$9,045	$11,380
7) Earned income tax credit	$3,110	$2,760
8) Food stamps	$3,768	$3,012
9) Disposable income (= rows 6 + 7 + 8)	$15,923	$17,152
10) Percentage of disposable income from wages (=row 6/row 9)	56.9%	66.3%
11) Total government subsidy (= rows 7 + 8)	$6,878	$5,722

what extent do low-wage workers use the government subsidies available to them?

We have assumed the low-wage family has four members, including two children and one wage-earner. Does this describe the average low-wage family? Our Los Angeles data set is too small to be reliable for such detailed descriptions, but we can get a sense of the relevant figures in examining data for the United States as a whole. According to the 1995 figures for the whole country, 42.3 percent of the workers earning below $7.25 are the only wage earner in their family. The av-

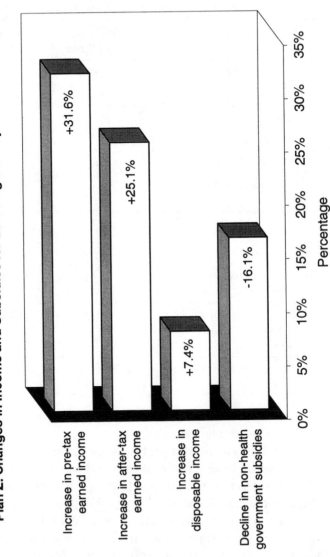

Figure 5.2
Plan Z: Changes in Income and Subsidies for Low-Wage Family After Ordinance

erage family size for a worker earning below $7.25 is 2.1 people. In other words, in more than half the families with a low-wage worker, there will be a second wage-earner in the family, and each wage-earner in the family is unlikely to be supporting two children.

But these results need to be considered in a broader context. The average low-wage worker in our data set earns $5.43 an hour under Plan Y and $4.94 under Plan Z. In either case, the average worker with a full-time job could not support a family of two at a level above the poverty line. This would obviously create severe difficulties for low-wage workers who wish to form families and to keep them intact. The intention of the living wage ordinance should therefore be precisely to give low-wage workers the opportunity to raise a family on the wages they earn. In fact, beyond the question of mere biological subsistence, this is the only meaning to the term "living wage" that has any integrity. This is why the family on which our are calculations are based—four people, one wage earner, two children—is an appropriate benchmark for measuring the benefits of the various living wage proposals.[3]

But do such low-wage families actually receive all the government support available to them, as our calculations have assumed? In their study for the City of Los Angeles in conjunction with the city's deliberations on its living wage ordinance, professors Douglas Williams and Richard Sander stated that, in fact, most poor families in Los Angeles do not take advantage of the subsidies available to them. In particular, with respect to the earned income tax credit (EITC), they write that "a majority of the Los Angeles residents who are eligible for the EITC do not know about it or do not use it."[4] Indeed, based on this claim, they argued that a relatively inexpensive city-directed information campaign to inform LA residents of their EITC entitlement would be a more effective way of reducing poverty than implementing a broad living wage ordinance.

However, the Williams and Sander study does not document their contention that fewer than half of eligible LA residents take advantage of the earned income tax credit. Moreover, the results from researchers on this subject provides strong evidence that this claim is wrong. For example, a rigorous 1994 study by the economist John Karl Scholz of the University of Wisconsin-Madison concludes that, for the United States as a whole, between 75 and 90 percent of those eligible do receive their benefits, with his best estimate of benefit recipients ranging being between 80 and 86 percent of those eligible. Scholz also finds that there are good reasons why most of the rest of those eligible for the EITC do not claim their entitlement—for example, they are either entitled to a smaller claim, or earn most of their living through self-employment or in household services occupations, and thus prefer not to file an income tax statement.[5]

However, even if Williams and Sanders's unsupported claim were true, it still would not follow that reliance on the EITC is an adequate substitute for a living wage ordinance. As the economists Barry Bluestone and Teresa Ghilarducci make clear, the EITC should properly be judged as a *complement* to an adequate minimum wage standard, not as a substitute for it. When an EITC program operates in conjunction with a below-poverty minimum wage, the EITC becomes a means of allowing businesses to continue offering only poverty wages, while shifting onto the public the costs of alleviating the poverty of even those holding full-time jobs.[6]

BENEFITS TO GOVERNMENT
OF SUBSIDY DECLINES

As the low-wage family comes to rely substantially less on government support to earn a living, the corollary is that government at various levels spends far less to help working people survive the effects of earning poverty wages. Table 5.3 documents the savings to the federal, state, and county governments in the case of the four-person, two-child family with one wage-earner, both under the Plan Y and Plan Z. As we see, based on our assumptions of family size, total government savings amounts to $4,391 per family under Plan Y, which, when multiplied by the number of workers affected under Plan Y–Narrow, comes to $14.6 million. With Plan Z, saving per family is $1,627, which multiplies to $1.2 billion when all 735,583 workers are considered.

As noted above, more than one-half of low-wage workers live in families where they are not the sole earner; and the average family size for such families is 2.1 persons, not four. Therefore, our estimates of government saving represent an upper-end figure, as families with more wage-earners and fewer or no children would not qualify to the same extent for the EITC, food stamps, or MediCal support. Such an upper-end estimate does, however, provide a sense of the orders of magnitude involved. Without trying to achieve a degree of precision with these estimates that is in any case unattainable, the actual figures for government saving are probably in the range of one-half of the total figures we have generated. Even if the actual total were one-third of our estimate, the saving to government would still be quite significant, especially given that such saving would be achieved without having to reduce the provision of any government services.

Table 5.3
Upper-End Estimated Saving to Government From Living Wage Ordinances
(Calculated for 4-person, 2-child family with one wage-earner)

	Plan Y (1) Saving per family	Plan Y (2) Saving for all families (column 1 x 3,355)	Plan Z (3) Saving per family	Plan Z (4) Saving for all families (column 3 x 735,583)
Federal government saving				
Higher income taxes	$521	$1.7 million	$521	$383.2 million
Lower EITC payments	$654	$2.2 million	$350	$257.5 million
Lower food stamp payments	$972	$3.2 million	$756	$556.1 million
Lower MediCal coverage	$625	$2.1 million	—	—
State government saving				
Lower MediCal coverage	$625	$2.1 million	—	—
Los Angeles County saving				
Less indigent health coverage	$994	$3.3 million	—	—
Total	$4,391	$14.6 million	$1,627	$1.2 billion

Given the existing structure of taxation and subsidies, it is unfortunate that the city governments—the entities that are implementing living wage ordinances—would not directly capture any of the savings from the decline in the low-wage families' reliance on government support. We see this in table 5.3 with our Los Angeles database. The table shows that all of the savings to government are received by the federal government, the California state government, and the Los Angeles County government, since these are the entities that either collect income taxes or finance the various subsistence programs to poor families. Given that the cities would be the entities creating savings for the other levels of government by establishing living wage ordinances, city officials could legitimately argue to federal, state, and county government representatives that they should receive a share of these living wage–generated benefits.

BENEFITS TO FIRMS

One of the most important developments in the recent economics literature is the finding that business firms can achieve substantial benefits when they pay their employees more than the market or law requires. This relatively new, but by now firmly established, perspective has important implications for assessing the potential impact of living wage ordinances.[7]

The previous view among economists held that when firms are forced to pay wages more than the market will bear, costly inefficiencies—such as underuse of relatively less skilled workers and overuse of capital equipment—would result. In this previous view, such inefficiencies would cause prices to rise and profits to fall, and would lead to higher unemployment, since workers with fewer skills would be unable to compete for jobs at the higher wage rate.

The more recent perspective has actually only rediscovered some old ideas that most economists had neglected for a generation. This perspective holds that when workers receive a higher wage, a firm benefits in many ways, including reduced labor turnover, better quality of work, better cooperation with management, more flexibility in the operation of a business, and higher overall morale.

Probably the most famous historical case illustrating these points was that of Ford Motor Company in the early part of this century. In 1913, the turnover rate at Ford Motors was roughly 400 percent. That means that Henry Ford found himself hiring four times the average number of workers he actually needed to staff production over the course of a year. Rates of absenteeism were similarly high. Recognizing this problem, Ford instituted the $5.00 a day wage rate for production workers, which amounted to a *near doubling* of wages at that time. It is now well documented in the professional literature that Ford's bold move led to significant decreases in both absenteeism and turnover. Other firms in this period, including Goodyear, General Electric, and Bethlehem Steel took slightly different, but equally dramatic, approaches in the attempt to reduce turnover and raise morale. These included profit-sharing arrangements, pension plans, health insurance, and educational subsidies for employees and their children. A careful analysis of these and related efforts demonstrates that they also produced significant changes in turnover and morale, which in turn brought gains in efficiency.[8]

These historical examples and the analytic literature that has developed around them are important evidence for assessing the potential impact of living wage initiatives and comparable interventions in the labor market. Once we allow for changes in worker morale and turnover, as well as other factors that will change a firm's productivity, it becomes easier to explain why minimum wage increases throughout the United States have not produced discernible employment losses or declines in efficiency. It can also help explain why more narrowly targeted laws for increasing wages, such as the provision in Baltimore, have also not produced the negative effects on employment and efficiency that older perspectives on such issues might have anticipated.

Many firms habitually try to keep wage payments as low as possible. But there are also many firms that pay their workers a wage well above the legal minimum, provide them with additional benefits, and still compete successfully in the marketplace. Such "high-wage" firms include many that compete directly with firms who pay minimum wages as much as possible. One of the benefits of living wage requirements is that they would induce many of these "low-wage" firms to operate along the high-wage path—providing direct benefits to the firms' workers, but also increasing the capacity of the firms to compete through creating a high-morale, low-turnover work environment.

To demonstrate these points more concretely, it will be useful to consider the operating procedures of some actual firms. Our colleague Prof. David Fairris, a distinguished labor economist, investigated the workplace practices of three high-wage firms in the Los Angeles area, in conjunction with our research on the Los Angeles living wage ordinance. The three firms that Fairris studied were Bell Industries, a large distributor of industrial equipment; All American Home Center, a home products store; and Rogers Poultry. We will also briefly contrast Prof. Fairris's findings on these firms with the operations of one (unnamed) firm that operates along the low-wage path, despite receiving substantial subsidies from the City of Los Angeles.

Bell Industries

Founded in the early 1950s, Bell Industries is the country's seventh-largest industrial distributor of electrical equipment, such as semiconductors. It is listed on the New York Stock Exchange, has roughly $700 million in annual sales, and roughly 1500 employees, full-time, nonunion workers.

The most prevalent low-skilled employees at Bell are warehouse workers, who started at a $7.00 per hour base wage as of September 1996. They also receive hourly incentive pay, yearly bonuses, and stock dividends (the company maintains a stock-purchase plan for all employees). Workers receive large amounts of training, not only in skills specific to the company but also in such general areas as computer literacy. There is little concern, though, that the company is training workers in general skills that their employees will put to use elsewhere. The reason is that with the high wages and benefits, there is very little turnover.

Theodore Williams, CEO of Bell Industries, said that the company's philosophy towards its workers "pays off."[9] He estimates that the company may spend roughly $10,000 on a new worker before that worker is able to produce at efficient levels. This includes recruitment costs, training, lost output while learning the job, and possible damage to equipment during the learning process. Under these circumstances, it benefits the company to pay workers well and to strive to retain them. Williams has learned in conversations with other CEOs—he cites the specific example of a discussion with management at the Bank of

America—that many companies are simply unaware of the costs they face with high worker turnover.

High turnover is not the only cost of a bad human resource policy, according to Williams. Employees that are mistreated by their employer often do not have the company's best interest in mind as they do their jobs. Williams' motto is "I want you [the employees] to treat me the way I treat you." This, in part, explains why the company remains non-union; Williams considers it a failure of management if a company becomes unionized. It is a sign that the management was not enlightened in the proper way to treat workers. Asked point-blank whether he truly believes that the high wage/good benefits/fair treatment of workers pays off in the form of higher profits, he responded, "Unquestionably."

All American Home Center

All American Home Center has roughly 250 employees, more than $25 million in annual sales, and a history of serving the community since 1959. Lanny Gertler is president and majority owner of All American. His firm faces competition from the likes of Home Depot and Home Base. Nevertheless, the firm has a long tradition of paying decent wages and benefits and treating its employees well.[10]

Of the workforce of 250, nearly half work part-time. However, virtually all promotion is entirely from within the company, so that all full-timers began as part-timers. All part-timers also have access to the same benefits packages as full-timers.

As of September 1996, unskilled, part-time workers starting at All American received $5.00 per hour, with the opportunity to reach $6.00 within six months and more than $7.50 within two years. The average part-timer earned $8.33 per hour, not counting overtime pay for any Sunday work, profit-sharing year-end bonuses (which, in 1994 amounted to roughly $1500 for part-timers and double that amount for full-timers), and various benefits. These include sick pay, paid holidays, medical insurance (two-thirds of the cost paid by the company), and two weeks' paid vacation a year for those with two years' service, rising to a month off with pay for those with five years' service.

Except for management positions, All American rarely hires from the outside for any position above part-time beginning "associate." Part-timers become part of a team within a department, and earn more in pay and benefits (e.g., the company contributes 80 percent of the health insurance premiums for full-timers) as they move up the skill ladder to full-timer (starting pay was $10 per hour plus overtime for Sunday as of September 1996), and then perhaps team leader and assistant department manager (who receive weekly bonuses ranging from $12 to $40 per week).

How, and why, does Gertler take such an approach toward his employees? He states unequivocally that "it pays off." Indeed, he believes "other firms are stupid for not paying more to their employees." He cites better worker morale and commitment to the company, which translates into better service for customers, higher productivity, and the virtual elimination of such problems as internal theft. (In general, roughly 50 percent of the theft faced by retail establishments is committed by its own employees.)

The other benefit, of course, is reduced turnover, which translates into reduced costs of training and recruitment. Company personnel documents reveal the average length of tenure with the company: the management staff has been with the company for an average of 16 years and the full-time staff, an average of 11 years. Part-timers are composed of students and others whose schedules require that they maintain a workweek of reduced length. This is the contingent workforce at most companies, referred to as "floaters"—workers with very high turnover and therefore an extremely low amount of time with the firm, typically measured in months, not years. At All American, the part-time workforce has been employed with the company for an average of 4.5 years, a remarkably long tenure for such employees.

Rogers Poultry

In business since 1927, Rogers Poultry is a south-central Los Angeles firm that does roughly $15 million in annual sales and employs about 60 full-time production workers. The Rogers workers are organized by the United Food and Commercial Workers, a union that has been at the plant for roughly a decade.[11]

The union is part of the explanation for the worker pay and benefit levels at Rogers—but only part of the explanation. The other major factor is the ethos of management, as put forth by owner Tracy Claus and Plant Director, Terry Carter. The evidence for this is that Rogers has wages and benefits far superior to its competitors, both union and nonunion, including some firms that are much larger and better-known.

As of September 1996, every production worker in the plant received $7.65 per hour regardless of job task. To equalize the pay per unit of effort or pay per hour of exposure to dangerous work, workers rotate through jobs in the plant (although this is not forced upon workers). Job rotation also has the advantage of reducing repetitive strain injuries to workers. The company pays 100 percent of workers' medical and dental insurance, which is extended, at no cost to the employee, to immediate family members. The company contributes 40 cents per hour into a pension fund. There are six paid holidays per year, three paid days of family leave, and paid vacations which last anywhere from two weeks for newer employees to five weeks for those with fifteen years' service.

The conditions of work seem extraordinarily good for a meat-processing plant. As is typical for this industry, it is quite cold on the plant floor. But the company provides workers with thermal socks, rubber boots, and coats, in addition to various forms of protective wear for workers in the more dangerous jobs. Plant director Terry Carter reports that there has not been an injury in the plant for more than a year. Overtime is never forced on workers, but many choose to work overtime in order to earn the time-and-a-half pay scale—1996 company records reveal that one of the more ambitious overtime workers earned close to $28,000 in additional wages in 1995. The hours and break periods are similar to those of its competitors. However, Rogers employees have much greater flexibility in timing their half-hour lunch or twenty minutes of break time. Moreover, Rogers workers may use the rest room at any time they please. Finally, Rogers workers have a number of amenities—drinking fountain, microwave, even a television in the break room— not found at their competitor firms.

How does Rogers compete? The answer, according to Terry Carter, is that the company has virtually no turnover, and that workers have a high regard for the company and the work they do. Low turnover means that the company can economize on training and recruitment costs. It also means that the workforce is an extremely capable and highly flexible unit. Thus, Rogers can cater to more finicky customers, such as Knotts Berry Farm theme park or Tony Roma's, the spare-rib restaurant chain, filling specialty orders of various kinds with high productivity and quality.

"No-Name Meats": A Sample Low-Wage Employer

The firm we consider for contrast—and which we will call "No-Name Meats" to protect its identity—is, like Rogers Poultry, in the meat-processing industry. Its product is not a direct competitor with Rogers, but the firm still operates under almost identical workplace and market conditions. The case of this firm is especially relevant to our analysis because, in the mid-1990s, it relocated into the City of Los Angeles proper from a neighboring community and has been receiving substantial city subsidies for making this move. Because No-Name Meats receives annual subsidies in excess of $100,000 for employment creation, its wage levels would have to comply with the standards set by the Los Angeles living wage ordinance (Plan Y).[12]

No-Name Meats currently employs roughly 200 workers, 150 of whom are classified as unskilled. The move to its new Los Angeles facility was projected to allow its workforce to double in size, with an even larger percentage of the new jobs coming from unskilled job classifications.

What are conditions like for workers at No-Name Meats? Interviews with workers conducted in 1995 reveal that the starting wage then was $4.25 per hour. There were no paid sick days or vacations, but the company did provide a minimal contribution towards health insurance for its workers. Work begins at 6:15 A.M. and ends at 2:30 P.M., during which time workers receive a fifteen-minute break at 8:45 and a half-hour lunch beginning at noon.

Interviews with workers reveal that they are routinely forced to work overtime and generally bothered by supervisors for their occasional need to use the rest room. The difficulties of working in the typically cold environment of a meat processing plant are worsened by the fact that the company does not provide warm clothing for its workers. In addition, female workers regularly report being discriminated against in their dealings with management. Finally, workers report that certain basic amenities—a drinking fountain, a microwave for heating up lunches—are missing.

Rogers Poultry and "No-Name Meats" typify the divisions between high-wage, high-productivity and low-wage, low-productivity management styles. There are many high-wage firms such as Rogers throughout the country that are thriving.[13] These firms report numerous benefits to themselves—reduced turnover, higher productivity and quality, greater flexibility in the deployment of workers, and enhanced cooperation with management—from treating their workers fairly and with respect. After the implementation of a living wage ordinance, firms that are forced out of the low-wage path should be able to capture at least some of the benefits from following the high-wage, high-productivity path.

It is unlikely, however, that the costs to some low-wage firms of being forced to pay higher wages would be completely offset by its benefits. This is especially true inasmuch as the professional literature on these benefits suggests that at least some of the gains to high-wage firms result precisely from their status as *relatively* more desirable workplaces. This means that when other firms are mandated to implement a living wage minimum, the initial high-wage firms could lose some of their advantages. Correspondingly, the formerly low-wage firms would not reap any productivity benefits through implementing the mandated raise. Nevertheless, the benefits to all firms of paying a living wage minimum, even if they do not fully offset the firms' added costs, are likely to be real and substantial.

Would Low-Wage Workers Be Replaced?

While firms are likely to become more productive due to a living wage mandate, would part of this change result through the firm attracting a new, more productive pool of workers through offering the higher wage? If so, would this new pool of workers take the jobs of the existing, presumably less productive low-wage workers? Were this the case, the living wage ordinance would be contributing unwittingly to the loss of employment for the very-low-wage workers it is seeking to help. Some analysts, such as professors Williams and Sander in their study for Los Angeles, believe that this would follow from the implementation of a living wage ordinance. We disagree, for several reasons.

First, replacing workers is costly to firms—in recruiting and training, for example. This will discourage firms from substituting a new set of workers for their existing employees. Moreover, it is unlikely that firms will reorganize their production processes, altering the technology and the skills and training required of workers, in reaction to the living wage. Hiring "better" workers is therefore most likely to mean simply hiring workers who work harder, and are more diligent and conscientious in their duties. In our view, a living wage minimum will, to a substantial degree, *create* this kind of behavior among the existing workforce as morale increases. That is, the existing workforce will become "better" workers upon receiving a living wage.

Second, even assuming such replacement does take place in limited amounts, it is not immediately clear what impact this will have on productivity and the wage structure in any given region. It is possible, of course, that some of the existing low-wage workers will transfer to jobs outside the scope of the living wage initiative, while other workers with better work habits will accept the newly mandated higher-wage jobs. But the higher-wage workers are unlikely to quit their existing jobs unless the living wage minimum is higher than the wage they are currently receiving. Meanwhile, the low-wage workers who would be displaced are unlikely to receive a *lower* wage in their new jobs than the one they were receiving before the living wage laws came into effect. As such, even if some displacement were to occur, the wages of low-paid workers in general should still rise through the living wage.

Empirical evidence from a related situation—when a firm first becomes a union shop from having been non-union—provides some useful guidance. After a union is organized and it bids up wages through collective bargaining, an employer has every incentive to replace its existing workers with new workers who possess greater skills and/or better work habits. If this were to happen, then there would be no wage improvement for union workers. Those earning union wages would be exactly the same more productive workers who would earn the higher wage even if they worked in non-union jobs. However, evidence shows that once differences in skills are accounted for, and after correcting for the possibility that there exists a tendency for workers to choose to work in a union firm precisely because they are more productive, we still find that workers in organized firms earn about 20 percent more than workers in non-union firms.[14] In this situation, in short, the higher wage earned by union workers results, to a significant degree, from the organizing efforts of union members, not just from the fact that more skilled workers have supplanted the less skilled in the union shop. The intervention of the union, in other words, does not lead to newly organized workers being displaced, but rather brings higher wages to those same workers. We anticipate that implementing a living wage ordinance would produce a similar pattern: the existing workers in the affected firms would not be displaced but would rather themselves enjoy the benefits of the living wage standard.

COMMUNITY BENEFITS

Increasing incomes for the families of low-wage workers generate community spillover effects. These include increased spending at local businesses, higher rates of home ownership, education, and opportunities for business investments by local residents; and, following from the other benefits, more robust housing and small-business markets in the low-income neighborhoods.

In conjunction with our study on Los Angeles, our colleague Prof. Gary Dymski conducted research on the size of this effect in some poorer communities. In estimating these effects, one has to allow that low-wage workers might in fact seek to leave a poor community once their incomes have been pushed above the poverty line. But beyond this, the extent of such community effects is mostly dependent on how many workers are affected by a given living wage ordinance. For example, in the ordinances we considered in which only firms doing business with the city are mandated to pay a living wage—Plan X and Plan Y—the number of workers receiving a raise would be tiny in proportion to the entire municipal economy. For example, even with Plan Y–Broad, the most extensive of the cases in which only firms holding city contracts are affected, the total number of workers getting raises is no more than 10,000. This constitutes less than 0.5 percent of the Los Angeles County labor force of 2.3 million. Even if these 10,000 workers are clustered in relatively few communities, the impact of their increased buying power within their communities would be modest. Dymski, for example, estimated that with a Plan Y–type ordinance, after workers came home with larger paychecks and spent a substantial share of this increased income within their own communities, over-all income in these selected communities would rise by roughly 0.6 percent.

While this number is small, it does also suggest that a Plan Z–type ordinance, which would affect about one-third of all workers in Los Angeles, could have quite dramatic effects within these same poorer communities. This again underscores the importance of considering the viability of large-scale living wage programs—of a Plan Y program on a countywide, statewide, or even national scale. This is the question to which we now turn in our concluding chapter.

6—Toward a National Living Wage Policy

STRENGTHS AND LIMITS OF MUNICIPAL LIVING WAGE LAWS

Municipal living wage programs work: that is the basic result that flows from the evidence we have compiled. We cannot assume that government agencies will enforce these ordinances. But if living wage supporters maintain vigilance, these programs will, most importantly, succeed in raising living standards for low-wage workers, such that a worker can hold a full-time job and raise a family. Even then, the family will be living right at the poverty line, and it would be far preferable to set the living wage minimum at a wage above the poverty line. But given the precipitous fall in the national minimum wage over the past thirty years, establishing a living wage minimum *at least* at the poverty line is a substantial step forward. Among other things, successful living wage campaigns create political momentum that can used to build support for more ambitious measures to eliminate low-wage poverty in the United States.

Living wage programs also work in ways that critics claim they fail. In almost all cases, they will not create undue cost burdens on businesses that would force businesses to lay off low-wage workers or relocate to avoid having to comply with the law. They also will not significantly raise the costs to city governments of providing basic services, which might then have even forced the cities to reduce spending on poverty alleviation. Contrary to the critics, in other words, living wage measures do not end up hurting the very people they intend to help.

Rather, the ordinances we have studied are affordable for the cities that would implement them and for the private businesses that would fall under their requirements. Most firms affected by citywide living wage ordinances—the "low-impact" firms in our sample—will face negligible increases in their costs. Surely in an environment of competitive bidding and productivity growth, these firms can find the means to absorb increases in production costs on the order of 1 percent or less. A relatively small number of firms will experience more substantial increases, of 10 percent or more of their total costs. But these increases can also readily be absorbed. Firms holding concession contracts with cities, such as restaurant outlets at airports, can raise their prices modestly, so that customers absorb part of the cost increase. High-impact firms that perform city services, such as child-care service providers, should be expected to pass on a significant portion of their added costs to the city through better contract terms. But even when they do pass on a share of their added costs, these new costs will represent so small a share of cities' budgets that they also can be readily absorbed.

In addition, the high-impact firms should also experience productivity gains, as turnover and absenteeism fall and morale on the job rises. At the same time, there is no reason to expect that living wage policies will lead to job losses and higher unemployment among low-wage workers. The evidence we reviewed in chapter 2 shows that increases in national and state minimum wage rates are not associated with higher unemployment, primarily because other factors, especially the overall level of demand for workers in the economy, will exert far greater influence than the minimum wage standard in determining the unemployment rate.

Finally, living wage policies work in helping to establish an alternative to the business subsidy policies that have dominated city politics for the past twenty years. Setting a living wage minimum for firms receiving contracts or subsidies with a city makes a clear statement that the types of firms the city should be trying to nurture are those that pay fair wages and compete through maintaining high workplace morale. The Los Angeles ordinance, among others, goes further, toward establishing that the city will not subsidize firms that pay poverty wages. A living wage minimum for contractors also reduces the incentive for cities to outsource their services to private contractors who make lowball winning bids by paying sub-poverty wages to their workers.

In short, the municipal living wage programs that are being debated and implemented around the country will work both in terms of their benefits and their costs. Moreover, reaching this conclusion does not depend on making heroic assumptions about how living wage policies would bring dramatic improvements in a local economy. In fact, the primary reason why living wage programs can work in terms of both benefits and costs is straightforward: its benefits are concentrated while its costs are diffused. That is, the main benefits of the policy will be concentrated among a relatively small number of workers and their families, while the costs can be readily diffused among a large number of affected firms, as well as, to a lesser extent, city governments and consumers.

But this conclusion forces us to consider another point. With most living wage ordinances, such as that in Milwaukee (on which Plan X was based) or Los Angeles (on which we based Plan Y), the number of people affected will be relatively small. Using our Los Angeles data base, even the most far-reaching Plan

Y–Broad scenario would provide direct wage increases for roughly 7,500 full- and part-time workers, which amounts to no more than 0.3 percent of the total workforce in Los Angeles of 2.3 million people. Perhaps another 10,000 will receive health benefits, paid days off, and indirect wage gains through the "ripple effect." This is not to denigrate the real and significant gains to these workers and their families, or the achievement of living wage proponents in getting such ordinances passed. But let us put these successes in a broader perspective. The overriding concern with which we began was not how to raise wages only for a small group of urban low-wage workers, but to contribute toward redressing the wage squeeze that most working people in the country have experienced over the past twenty-five years. Considered on their own, the Milwaukee or Los Angeles–type measures will make only a small contribution toward reversing the economy-wide wage squeeze.

Of course, Plan Z, based on defeated 1996 proposals in both Denver and Houston, would provide much more widespread benefits. This kind of countywide wage minimum would mean raises for about 870,000 full- and part-time workers in the context of Los Angeles County, more than one-third of the county's workforce. But on a per-worker basis, the benefits of Plan Z are substantially more limited than those associated with Plan Y. In Plan Z, as with Plan X, the "living wage" worker with a full-time job would still receive an annual income 19 percent below the poverty rate for a family of four and would still not be assured of either private health insurance or any paid days off.

The national minimum wage rate has the broadest coverage, but achieves the least in terms of getting low-wage workers a raise. Even with the raise to $5.15 an hour as of September 1997, a full-time worker earning that minimum is still 18 percent below the poverty-line income for a family of three and 36 percent below the four-person family poverty line. The proposal of Senator Kennedy and Representative Bonior to increase the minimum wage to $7.25 by 2002 in five annual steps would make significant progress toward eliminating the poverty-wage minimum. However, even in 1997, a $7.25 wage for a full-time worker will generate a sub–poverty line income level for a four-person family; so with inflation, the year-end earnings of a full-time worker at $7.25 per hour by 2002 would be well below the poverty line.

Let us consider, then, a more ambitious aim: to create a living wage policy with terms similar to Plan Y—$7.25 an hour in 1997 dollars plus benefits and paid days off—but with a scope similar to Plan Z, or better still, a national scope. The question is, under what conditions could a Plan Y–type package realistically serve as a model for a regional or national minimum wage policy?

ENDING ROBIN HOOD IN REVERSE

Since the minimum wage peaked in 1968 at $7.37 (in 1997 dollars), not only has the real value of the minimum wage been falling, but the gap has grown more generally between the rich and poor. Between 1968 and 1994, the real incomes of the wealthiest 5 percent of households rose by more than 60 percent—from $119,189 to $183,044—while the minimum wage was falling by 30 percent. So on the simplest level, a national or regional $7.25 minimum is realistic, since all the raises to workers earning below $7.25 could be paid for through reducing the incomes of the top five percent of families from $183,944 to $154,490. The richest 5 percent of households would still have incomes 35 percent above their 1968 level, and their privileged lifestyles would change little. Or to carry out this logic a bit further down the household income distribution: given 1994 income levels, if we were to redistribute income from the richest 20 percent of households to pay for the raises needed to bring all low-wage workers up to a $7.25 minimum, these wealthiest 20 percent of households would experience an income decline of only 6.7 percent, from $105,945 to $98,873. Again, in other words, such a redistribution would not make a serious dent in the lifestyles of the most affluent households.

Of course, such redistributive schemes are only illustrative exercises, suggesting the resources that are available if the country were committed to ending low-wage poverty. But such exercises do not take any account of the ways the economy has changed over the past thirty years, or ways that it might have changed had the distribution of income been more egalitarian over these years.

As we saw in chapter 2, if the minimum wage had been rising at just the rate of productivity growth from 1968 until today—that is, with low-wage workers' incomes buying a constant share of the economy's increasing production of goods and services, but no more—then the minimum wage in 1997 would be $11.20. The real question then is, given that a $7.37 national minimum wage was the law in 1968, what has changed so dramatically about the U.S. economy since then that could have caused the precipitous fall in the minimum wage? Why, in other words, was $7.37 the actual minimum wage in 1968 but seemingly beyond our reach in 1998? Answering that question should then also provide an illuminating perspective on what needs to change about the U.S. economy today to make a $7.25 national mimimum a viable policy.

THE "GOLDEN" AND "LEADEN"
AGES OF THE POSTWAR ECONOMY

To begin with, there is one way in which the U.S. economy circa 1968 and 1997 were similar. It is that unemployment was very low in both years by historical standards. In 1968, unemployment was 3.6 percent while in 1997, it was 4.8 percent. The full percentage point difference between the two years is, of course, substantial, amounting to 1.4 million more unemployed workers in terms of the the 1997 labor market. But both figures still contrast sharply with the average unemployment rate of 5.8 percent between 1950 and 1997.

But this similarity only makes it more difficult to understand why the $7.37 national minimum wage rate in 1968 was 30 percent higher than the $5.15 minimum that prevailed by the end of 1997. In fact, some crucial differences between the two periods are evident even from the most basic statistics. One is that while unemployment was low by historical standards in both periods, that full percentage point difference—specifically that unemployment fell below a 4 percent threshold in 1968—was significant in giving workers more bargaining power in setting wage rates. In addition, unemployment was quite low throughout the second half of the 1960s, averaging 3.8 percent between 1965 and 1969. For the five-year period 1993–97, unemployment averaged 5.8 percent, basically equal to the long-run average rate.

More generally, the average rate of economic growth (i.e., growth of Gross Domestic Product) was far higher in the late 1960s, averaging a remarkable 4.7 percent per year between 1965 and 1969, as opposed to a 2.7 percent growth rate between 1993 and 1997 (through the first three quarters of 1997). For growth to accelerate depends on two factors. The first is that more people be working, and we have already seen how far unemployment had fallen in the second half of the 1960s. The second factor is that productivity on the job be increasing. As with the 3.8 unemployment rate of 1965–69, we see a far better productivity performance between 1965 and 1969, averaging 2.1 percent per year, than 1993–97, when productivity grew by slightly more than 1 percent per year.

Figures of this sort make clear why the late 1960s are widely considered to be the crowing period of what has been termed the "golden age" of the U.S. economy. The golden age, lasting roughly from the end of World War II through the 1960s, was characterized by rapid economic growth, low unemployment, mild business cycles, and rising living standards, especially for the white male sector of the working class. By contrast, we may broadly characterize the period since the early 1970s as the U.S. economy's "leaden age," in that it has been distinguished by slow growth, high unemployment, more severe business cycles, and stagnating or declining living standards for the majority.

What lay behind the golden age, in particular the years of peak performance in the second half of the 1960s; and what brought on the leaden age that we have experienced for the past twenty-five years?[1]

Part of the golden age boom resulted from the fact that the United States was still the unquestioned leader in producing manufactured goods for exports. U.S. exports were also greatly bolstered by dramatic policy initiatives, such as Marshall Plan financing of European reconstruction after World War II and the postwar development of the Bretton Woods monetary system, which led to the creation of the International Monetary Fund and the World Bank. Both the Marshall Plan and the Bretton Woods monetary system were committed to promoting a U.S.-led free-trade regime throughout the capitalist world.

But on top of these general factors, two deliberate policy actions were responsible for increasing growth and pushing the unemployment rate so low by the second half of the 1960s. The first factor was the deliberate initiative of the Kennedy and then Johnson administrations. In the U.S. and elsewhere in the West, full employment programs were considered necessary to counteract the claims to superiority coming from the Soviet Union. After all, Nikita Khruschev's 1956 boast that the Soviet economy would "bury" the West was then taken quite seriously, since the Soviet economy experienced no unemployment when the capitalist economies fell into depression in the 1930s and then grew at more than double the U.S. rate throughout the 1950s.

Thus, President Kennedy first proposed and, in 1964, President Johnson got through Congress a program to cut taxes sharply without reducing government spending. The decline in tax revenues would increase the federal deficit, but the extra after-tax income that households would enjoy would encourage them to spend more. This extra spending would in turn create more jobs.

However, over and above this deliberate effort at expansion came the decision by the Johnson administration to dramatically escalate spending on the Vietnam War. Defense spending jumped by $11 billion over a nine-month period beginning in July 1965, an almost 10 percent increase in all federal spending. Of course, the most important fact about the Vietnam War was that it was a brutal imperialist adventure. But in terms of its impact on the domestic economy, the Vietnam escalation, coming on top of the

Kennedy/Johnson tax cuts, stimulated economic growth and job opportunities beyond a point that had been experienced at any time since World War II.

The tight labor market conditions led businesses to become more aggressive in their methods of recruiting workers, but they did adapt with time. In April 1966, *Business Week* reported that "US employers are finding that the tight market for labor is forcing them to use gimmicks to lure sorely needed workers from other companies—and other countries as well." Among the specific strategies employed, the story noted that "Ford and other employers have combed Appalachia and the Ozarks, looking for workers among coon and squirrel hunters. They've come up with, at most, a handful." However, by February 1968, *Business Week* ran a story headlined "A Tight Labor Market that Doesn't Really Hurt," that described "the proved talent of business for living in a tight labor market." It reported that "after three years with unemployment near or below 4 percent, business knows how to get the labor it needs." The story detailed ways in which businesses were increasingly recruiting women, blacks, and other minorities; expanding their job training programs; and providing more opportunities and incentives for promotion.

Inflation in the 1960s

Despite the striking economic achievements in the second half of the 1960s, almost all mainstream economists today contend that government interventions in this period were a failure. Their argument is that the 1960s expansionary policies set off inflationary pressures which were uncontrollable, eventually producing the stagflation—stagnating real growth accompanied by persistent inflation—that characterized the 1970s. Indeed, both liberal and conservative economists persistently return to this argument in explaining why, in today's economy, the government must be ever vigilant in preventing unemployment from falling so low that workers can win higher wages, which in turn will encourage price increases. But how serious were the problems of inflation then?

Inflation did rise over this period, from an average of 1.2 percent in 1960 to 1964 to 3.9 percent in 1965 to 1969. However, average real incomes and employment conditions did not worsen but *improved* as the inflation rate notched upward in the second half of the 1960s. But what even this relatively moderate increase in inflation did then, as it does now, was to redistribute income. In particular, when creditors are owed a fixed amount of dollars to be paid over a number of years, the real value of this fixed amount of dollars diminishes as the buying power of the dollar falls with inflation. Thus creditors, who are disproportionately wealthy, lose in inflation while debtors, who are disproportionately non-wealthy, benefit. This explains the adamant opposition of Wall Street today to declining unemployment rates that might then produce an uptick in the inflation rate, a point to which we return shortly.

Nevertheless, inflation had not reached a high level by the late 1960s, and in particular, there is no evidence that it had inhibited economic growth or job creation. But if inflation was not the primary factor leading to the disintegration of the "golden age" economic performance of the 1960s, then what was? We can point to four interrelated influences: globalization, "financialization" of the economy, labor market changes, and rising inequality.

Globalization

Since the 1960s, U.S. firms have faced far greater competition in world markets. Indeed, profitability in the

United States had already begun to decline by the late 1960s because of the rise of German and Japanese manufacturing competition. By 1971, the United States ran its first trade deficit of the post–World War II era—buying more from other countries in imports than we sold to them in exports—and it has run a trade deficit every year since 1974.

The internationalization of the U.S economy has also increased the outflow of foreign investment from the United States. Foreign investment by U.S. companies has risen steadily since the 1970s, reaching $298 billion in 1995. This amounted to more than 29 percent of gross domestic investment by private firms in that year—U.S. firms, in other words, invested nearly 30 cents abroad for every dollar invested domestically.

There is an extensive debate on the extent to which globalization in the form of increased trade integration and foreign investment by U.S. firms has led to depressed U.S. wages. The general view is that it has had some impact, but there is widespread disagreement as to how serious that impact has been. Among other factors suggesting that the effects might not be serious is that most U.S. trade as well as most foreign investment is not with low-wage countries, but with countries whose wage levels are similar to our own. However, this view of the matter leaves out an important dimension of the situation, which is the power globalization has conferred to businesses in terms of their increased capacity to *threaten* U.S. workers. The following recent examples illustrate this power:

- 4,000 workers at a Xerox plant in Webster, New York, accepted 33 percent cuts in base pay to avoid a threatened plant closure. Union leaders expressed a belief that the plant would move to Mexico or Asia if wages weren't cut.
- National Service Industries threatened to move 300 jobs from its lighting plant in Lithonia, Georgia unless workers

took a cut of 20 percent in pay and 36 percent in benefits. The company has been investigating production in Mexico, though the jobs in question would move to another plant in Georgia with lower labor costs.

- Workers at a Leviton Co. plant in Warwick, Rhode Island agreed to freeze wages and work twelve-hour shifts without overtime pay because the company threatened to move production of electrical outlets to Mexico.

This threat effect is difficult, if not impossible to measure with statistics. But it is easy to see how it can exert substantial downward pressure on wages.[2]

In addition, the global integration of the U.S. economy has made it more difficult for the government to pursue a 1960s-style, full-employment, expansionary policy, assuming the political will existed to attempt such a program. The problem is that a high proportion of the increased spending resulting from an expansionary program will be spent on imports, so that fewer new jobs will be created in the United States. Indeed, recent estimates find that 30 cents of every new dollar of income earned in the United States would be spent on imports.

Financialization

Here we are referring to the enormous expansion since the 1960s of speculative financial markets, both within the United States and again, in the integration of the U.S. and global markets. These include stock, bond, and foreign currency markets, but also "derivative" markets—i.e., the trading of future and optional claims on stocks, bonds, and foreign currencies. Consider one indicator of the enormous expansion of this area. In 1968, the total value of trading on the New York Stock Exchange was 26.6 times greater than the national GDP—that is, for every new dollar of goods and services produced in 1960, $26.60 worth of shares of existing corporations were traded on the New York Stock Exchange. By the end of 1996, the value of New York Stock Exchange trading had exploded to $878.10 for every dollar of new goods and services produced in the United States—a phenomenal increase since 1968 of 3,200 percent. But even this figure for the growth of trading on the New York Stock Exchange understates the actual growth of financial trading since the 1960s, since the growth in bond trading, foreign exchange, and derivatives has been even more rapid than that for the New York Stock Exchange.

What has been the effect of these financial trends on the overall economy, and in particular, on wages? First, the expansion of highly speculative financial markets has imparted a short-term bias to corporate managers. They are constantly under pressure to impress Wall Street with quarterly earnings. Therefore, they are less able to pursue policies that would entail initial investments in their workforce but would yield long-term productivity benefits. The obvious example here would be paying higher wages that would cut into immediate quarterly earnings, but over time, would produce a higher-morale workforce that would raise productivity.

The relative growth of speculative markets has also shifted the goals of macroeconomic policy. With financial markets becoming increasingly influential in the economy, the primary policy goal, especially of the Federal Reserve, has become to avoid inflation. This means protecting the value of assets traded on Wall Street rather than expanding the production of new goods and services, which in turn would bring more demand for workers and better prospects for wage increases.

Labor Market Changes

It has long been established that workers who are union members earn a wage rate about 20 percent higher than non-union workers, and even larger premiums when benefits are also taken into account. It therefore follows that wages would suffer a decline when unionization rates decline. The decline in unionization rates has been dramatic since the mid-1950s. Union representation reached its postwar peak in 1954 at the time of the merger of the AFL-CIO, when roughly 35 percent of all nonfarm workers belonged to unions. From 1954 through the early 1970s, union membership declined slowly, falling to 26 percent of nonfarm employment by 1973.

However, this decline in union membership accelerated as businesses began feeling the squeeze on profitability coming from international competition. Indeed, corporations began a deliberate offensive against unions in the 1970s. In 1978, Douglas Fraser, then president of the United Auto Workers, described management's offensive against unions as a "one-sided class war" on the part of business. By 1985, management consultant Richard I. Lyles claimed that "unions are on their way out. Twenty-first century historians will look back on this time right now—let's say from about 1982 to the mid-1990s—and they will call it the Management Revolution." By 1994, Aaron Bernstein's assessment in *Business Week* was that "Over the past dozen years, U.S. industry has conducted one of the most successful antiunion wars ever, illegally firing thousands of workers for exercising their rights to organize."

Unions have been fighting back since the mid-1990s, as symbolized by the election of a more aggressive leadership at the AFL-CIO in 1995, the victory of the Teamsters' union in its strike against United Parcel Service in the summer of 1997, and indeed, by the union movement's efforts in behalf of living wage campaigns throughout the country. Nevertheless, unionization rates have continued to decline, with only 14.5 percent of all workers, and 10.2 percent of private sector workers, belonging to unions as of 1996.[3]

The overall effect of this dramatic drop in union membership, of course, is that the wage and benefit gains workers receive through becoming union members is available to a declining share of the workforce. Declining minimum wages thus becomes one effect of businesses' "one-sided class war" against unions.

Since the 1980s, growing numbers of workers have also been placed in highly insecure work situations—without benefits, protection against dismissal, or, more generally, a modicum of job security. These workers constitute what has come to be termed the "contingent" labor market. The Bureau of Labor Statistics defines contingent workers as those "who do not perceive themselves as having an explicit or implicit contract for ongoing employment," with the definition of "ongoing employment" being at least one year.

There have been several attempts at measuring the numbers of contingent workers, but these estimates vary widely, depending on which categories of workers are included. The core group of contingent workers would include full-time employees who expect their jobs to last for a year, involuntary part-time employees, and those who involuntarily work as independent contractors, on-call workers, and day laborers, including people working in temporary-help agencies such as Kelly Services or Manpower Inc.

According to the Labor Department's careful study in Febrary 1995, these groups total approximately 10 percent of the U.S. labor force. These workers are hardly in a situation to bargain for higher wages. As such, their job insecurity has exerted significant downward pressure on wages.

Inequality and Stagnation

The changes in the economy since the 1960s have contributed both to declining growth and greater inequality. But inequality and stagnating growth also feed off each other. For one thing, greater inequality makes it more difficult for government policy to try to stimulate growth as presidents Kennedy and Johnson did in the 1960s. This is because when the wealthy get an additional dollar of income, they will spend only 70 cents of it. Therefore only that 70 cents will go immediately toward expanding the economy and creating more jobs. The wealthy will also then tend to put their other 30 cents of new income in speculative financial markets, thereby reinforcing the problems due to financialization. By contrast, a non-wealthy person will spend almost all of the extra dollar she receives, so that more economic growth and jobs are created quickly. An expansionary program will therefore have a more stimulative effect when the income distribution is more equal. Part of the reason why the large federal deficits incurred during the Reagan presidency did not lead to a strong economic expansion is precisely because the extra income went disproportionately to the rich, who in turn moved a large fraction of the funds into speculative financial activities.

CREATING FERTILE CONDITIONS FOR RISING WAGES

Some of the changes in the economy that have occurred since the late 1960s have been inevitable. It is not surprising, in retrospect, that between the 1960s and 1990s the U.S. economy became increasingly integrated with the rest of the world. On the other hand, the attack by business on unionism was conscious and premeditated—hardly the result of some impersonal economic force. But when we add up all the economic changes since the 1960s, the overarching point is this: there is nothing about our situation today that *requires* that the minimum wage be 30 percent below what it was in 1968, or that the average nonsupervisory worker earn 19 percent below what she or he could have made in 1972. Living wage supporters throughout the country have made clear that we are not helpless before these changes in our economic circumstances. But in addition to establishing a living wage minimum, what other kinds of policies would be supportive of rising wage levels, in particular for low-wage workers?

We can point to two main changes that need to occur: increasing the economy's growth rate to a level closer to that of the 1960s; and creating an environment in which the benefits of higher growth are shared in a much more equitable fashion. What types of policies in addition to a living wage minimum would be most effective at advancing these ends?

Increasing Growth

As discussed earlier, the economy's growth rate is well below its long-term trend. The average growth rate between 1990 and 1997 of about 2.1 percent per year pales alongside the remarkable 4.4 percent growth performance of the 1960s. But even during the leaden age decades of the 1970s and 1980s, growth averaged 3.0 percent per year. For the thirty-year period 1950–89, the average annual growth rate was 3.4 percent.

In the contemporary economy, the difference between a 2.0 and 3.0 percent average annual growth
rate is formidable. If we assume that over the decade
1997–2006 the economy were to grow at 3 percent on
average rather than at 2 percent, this would yield an
additional $4.7 trillion dollars in national income, an
average of $470 billion per year.

This would provide a generous fund from which to
raise the minimum wage to a living wage standard as
well as reduce unemployment dramatically. The following simple scenario illustrates this point. We assume that the economy is growing at 3 percent per
year from 1997 to 2006, while the labor force grows at
1.5 percent per year and the unemployment rate is
pushed down to an average of 4 percent per year. In
addition, the proportion of the labor force earning an
hourly wage of $7.25 or below remains stable over this
period at its 1997 level of about 30 percent of all
workers.

In this scenario, we then allow that all workers earning below $7.25 are given a raise up to the new $7.25
minimum. That would entail an average annual wage
increase for these workers of $3,700 (since the current average wage for those earning below $7.25 is
$5.40, and we continue to assume that a full-time job
amounts to 2,000 hours of work per year). For all
low-wage workers, the total raise would then amount
to $155 billion.

When this increase in the minimum wage occurs in
an economy growing at 3 percent rather than 2 percent, the additional 1 percent of growth would still
leave $315 billion in additional raises to be distributed
both as higher wages for the rest of the employed
labor force as well as in benefits for the 4 percent of
the labor force that is unemployed. Again, dividing
these shares of the growth dividend equally, the aver-

age annual income increase for the seventy percent of the work force earning above $7.25, as well as the four percent who are unemployed, would still be more than $3,000 per person. This, again, is *on top of* the gains they would all otherwise get with the economy growing at the 1990–97 average growth rate of about 2 percent. In short, in terms of establishing a living wage minimum, there is much at stake in trying to raise the economy's growth rate, if not to the 4.4 percent level of the 1960s, then at least to the 3 percent level of the 1970s and 1980s.

Expansionary Policies Again

Globalization, financialization, and the upward redistribution of income have made it more difficult for 1960s-style expansionary policies to succeed. But this does not mean that expansionary policy should be tossed aside as a policy tool. This is because, within a relatively short time period, expansionary policy is the only way of raising the economy's growth rate to a 3 percent average, and thus providing a large dividend to finance wage increases for both low-wage workers as well as the rest of the workforce. But even if we allow that the more fundamental economic challenges before us are longer term—such as dramatically reducing military expenditures or a creating more environmentally benign production system—the most equitable way of addressing these long-term problems is within a context of a more rapidly growing economy, not one where jobs are scarce and livelihoods threatened. This means that expansionary policy should not be abandoned, but rather that it should be targeted so that it also addresses the barriers to its success due to globalization, financialization, and upward income redistribution.

A successful expansionary policy in the contemporary environment hinges on addressing four questions: what should expand; how should the expansion be paid for; how to avoid rising inflation while wages are rising and unemployment is low; and how to distribute benefits of expansion fairly. Let us consider these in turn.

What Should Expand?

The 1960s expansion was led by two sectors. The Kennedy/Johnson tax cut produced an immediate growth in private consumption. The Vietnam escalation then led to a rise in military spending. Neither of these are desirable as leading growth sectors today. An expansion led by private consumption will mean that much of the initial thrust of the initiative will go to purchasing imports rather than stimulating domestic U.S. production and jobs. Increasing the military budget is an absurdity in the post–Cold War world.

The most appropriate target on which to focus an expansionary program is public investment, on improving the country's public transportation infrastructure and on education, health, child welfare, and environmental protection. Tremendous social and economic benefits would first of all flow from such spending. Productivity would rise, especially through the improvements in infrastructure and the investments in education. The benefits of productivity growth would also be equitably distributed, given that health care, education, support for children and the environment are all areas where the non-wealthy have been underserved for a generation. In addition, almost all of the new jobs created through expanding these programs would be stable full-time jobs within the United States itself. This is not to say that private consumption or investment or imports wouldn't also grow along with a jobs program focused on public investment. Indeed, because of the relatively strong expansion of domestic jobs and incomes coming from a public investment expansion—that is, precisely because public investment is an efficient focal point for expansion—its final effect will be to still create more private consumption, investment, and imports.

How to Pay for the Expansion

Wouldn't an expansionary policy entail increasing the deficit, as it did in the 1960s? Expansionary policy and deficit spending are so closely associated that they are often equated. A logical link does exist between expansionary policy and deficit spending, since a government that spends more than it receives in taxes will create more jobs when the economy is suffering from high unemployment. However, persistent deficit spending also leaves a heavy residue of interest payments. The U.S. government today spends 15 cents of every dollar of its budget on interest payments, which go mainly to wealthy individuals, big businesses, and banks. This is money that could be spent on schools, health or the environment, and it is more than double the amount spent on interest prior to the Reagan administration. Deficit spending should not therefore be considered as an inherently beneficent source of funds for increasing growth and raising living standards, but rather as one alternative that can be combined with others.

One way to finance a full-employment program without increasing the deficit is to change the way we are taxed so that the new tax structure better addresses the problems of globalization, financialization, and upward income redistribution. The most obvious place to begin here is to raise taxes on the wealthy, by instituting a wealth tax or increasing the progressivity of the existing income tax. Prof. Edward Wolff has examined the possibilities for a wealth tax in the United States in his 1995 book *Top Heavy* (New York: The New Press). He proposes a modest wealth tax modeled on that in Switzerland, in which only wealth greater than $100,000 is taxed, the tax rate would rise to a maximum of 1 percent of wealth, and this maximum rate would apply only to the richest 0.3 percent of the population. Wolff estimates that even such a modest tax would generate roughly $40 billion in annual revenues. These funds alone could finance a relatively small, though still effective, public investment program. Such a tax would also redistribute income downward by a small amount, as well as reduce the amount of money that the wealthy put into speculation.

Another tax policy change would be to eliminate the payroll tax that finances Social Security and Medicare, and to fund these programs out of the income tax or a newly instituted wealth tax. From the standpoint of promoting economic growth and especially establishing a living wage minimum, the payroll tax has two fundamental drawbacks. The first is that it raises the costs of employment and therefore discourages businesses from hiring more workers. The payroll tax also falls disproportionately on the non-wealthy, in that only the first $65,400 of wage and salary income is taxed. Wage and salary income above that amount is exempt, as is all of profit, interest, capital gain, and dividend income.

Another tax plan that would be even more effective in reducing financial speculation would be to tax security trading directly. Such a tax has been used frequently in many countries, and was proposed for the United States by the Bush administration soon after the 1987 stock market crash. The rate on such a tax could be set according to whether the country's priority is to raise revenue or discourage speculation. But both ends can also be accomplished at the same time. For example, consider the case in which a tax of only 0.5 percent is imposed on the value of each stock trade—that is if $100 in stock is traded, the tax on the trade would be 50 cents. The rate of taxation would then be scaled down appropriately by maturity for all bonds and derivative instruments, so that, for example, the tax on trading a one-year bond worth $100 would be only one cent. One of us, along with Dean Baker and Marc Schaberg, has estimated that even if such a tax were to reduce financial market trading by an unlikely 50 percent, the tax would still raise more than $30 billion annually in new revenue.[4] There are several challenging issues involved in making such a tax workable, the most important of which is designing it in such a way that domestic taxpayers cannot avoid the tax by moving their trading to alternative domestic markets or offshore. But such problems are not insurmountable, as experiences in Great Britain, Japan, and elsewhere have shown.

A final and perhaps most evident tax policy change for supporting public investments would be to reduce the myriad tax loopholes that do little or nothing to promote economic growth, while almost always contributing to an even more unequal income distribution. In chapter 3 we considered the cases of tax-exempt Industrial Revenue Bonds and the tax abatements offered through enterprise zones. We saw that, between these two programs alone, roughly $1.5 billion per year of tax revenues is now lost, while these programs have not been effective at promoting jobs or improving conditions in poor urban neighborhoods. But the costs of these programs is small relative to other "tax expenditures" that do not promote economic growth or a more equal income distribution.

Revenues roughly on the order of the wealth tax or a securities trading tax—$30–40 billion per year—could be raised through scaling back deductions for items such as capital depreciation and mortgage interest payments, which could then be used to promote a public investment–led growth program.

Tax policies aside, there is another way to pay for an expansionary program without increasing the federal deficit, which is for the Federal Reserve to increase the supply of credit in the economy. This, indeed, is the most common policy now deployed by the government to moderate business cycle fluctuations. But the government now uses this tool strictly to try to raise or lower interest rates in relatively small increments. This does nothing to address the problems of globalization, financialization, and upward income redistribution, and therefore has limited effectiveness. But the same technique of expanding the supply of credit could be used more effectively if the newly created funds were specifically targeted to finance, for example, a public investment program. The government would then issue bonds to pay for the new public investments and the Federal Reserve itself would buy these bonds.

How to Avoid Increasing Inflation

Government policies can address the arbitrary redistributive effects of inflation while still promoting wage increases and job growth. One way to do this is for workers and businesses to agree to limits on their wage and profit increases while the economy expands, the official term for such efforts being "incomes policies." However, for such policies to be acceptable to working people, the beginning point of bargaining would need to be that the distribution of income should become more equal. In this regard, it is important to recognize that workers are never directly responsible for the inflation which results from declining unemployment rates. By definition, inflation occurs only after businesses raise prices on their products. Of course, when unemployment is low, the presumption is that workers gain more bargaining power. Wages consequently rise, and businesses respond by increasing prices. But after a generation in which wages have been stagnating or declining for most workers, it certainly shouldn't be assumed that the goal of an incomes policy should be to freeze the existing income distribution in order to prevent inflation.

The other way to address the redistributive effects of inflation is to adjust the repayment of debts according to changes in the inflation rate, just as, for example, Social Security checks are now automatically adjusted for inflation. This way, the value of financial assets that are fixed in dollar terms would no longer depreciate through inflation. It is true that debtors would no longer benefit relative to creditors from increases in inflation, which would thereby foreclose one potential means of equalizing the country's income distribution. Still, supporters of a more egalitarian society should count not on inflation but rather on successful movements for higher wages, more public investment, and full employment in establishing a sustainable path toward greater equality. The Clinton administration's recent decision to begin issuing government bonds that are indexed to the inflation rate should therefore be regarded as a favorable development. This, along with similar measures within the private bond market, might begin to soften Wall Street's opposition to an expansionary program.

Labor Relations

While such a program would be important in raising the economy's growth rate and in sharing the benefits of growth more equitably, it still would be essential that the recent positive developments in the union movement begin to bear fruit—in particular through increases in the proportion of workers joining unions—if workers are going to receive their fair share of the growing economy. As an important step toward this end, workers must be able to choose whether to join a union in an environment free of intimidation. In a 1994 representative survey of working people, roughly one-third of non-union private-sector workers said they would vote for a union "if an election were held today." It is true that two-thirds said they preferred not to join a union. But the one-third who would like to join amounts to 30 million private sector workers who do not have the representation they desire.

Why aren't these 30 million workers represented by a union? The most evident reason is that workers do, in fact, face intimidation when they seek to organize. In the same survey noted above, 79 percent of respondents said it is likely that employees who seek union representation will lose their jobs, and 41 percent of non-union workers say they think they might lose their own jobs if they tried to organize. When workers file complaints about unfair labor practices, government officials have been inclined to rule against them. Even when workers win union representation, companies often stall and effectively refuse to negotiate a contract in good faith. Roughly a third of workplaces in which workers vote for union representation still do not finalize a collective bargaining contract with their companies.

Changing union election procedures would itself go far toward defending workers' rights to organize and thwarting companies' opportunities for stalling, disruption, and intimidation. One proposal, by the late

Prof. David Gordon of the New School for Social Research, would mandate automatic certification of union representation upon a 55 percent majority of workers signing union membership cards. A variation on this was proposed by a federal government–sponsored commission led by the labor economist and former Labor Secretary John Dunlop. It would require elections within five days of submission of signed petitions.[5]

Finally, it is important to recognize that union representation can also make a significant contribution toward a sustainable expansionary policy. In particular, incomes policies can be most effectively accomplished within the structure of collective bargaining, especially, of course, if some degree of cooperation can be created between the bargaining parties.

Creating High-Productivity Workplaces

To achieve a rate of economic growth of at least 3 percent, and thus an environment most conducive for minimum wage increases, will require that more workers have jobs, but also that productivity on the job increases. As we have argued, part of this productivity increase will result simply through paying the higher wages themselves, as turnover and absenteeism decline and worker morale rises. Public investments in education and infrastructure will also raise productivity growth. But, as was suggested through the experiences of Bell Industries, All American Home Center and Rogers Poultry discussed in chapter 5, productivity can be enhanced further through promoting a cooperative work environment.

However, there are significant initial start-up investments necessary to create cooperation on the job, even while recognizing that these start-up costs lead to long-term productivity gains. As we saw in part with the three Los Angeles firms, establishing a cooperative workplace does entail higher wages and benefits, but it also means creating solid opportunities for promotion; a non-alienating physical environment; and genuine authority for workers in determining how the work process is organized.

Such a transformation of a workplace environment would not normally be evaluated favorably by financial markets. This is in part the result of the general short-term bias emanating from the exponential increase in speculative financial practices in U.S. markets. But in addition, both business managers and financial market analysts take a skeptical view of arrangements through which managers are asked to transfer some of their shop-floor power to workers. Thus, a 1995 survey of senior line and human resource executives at mid-sized and large U.S. companies found that 98 percent of respondents agreed that improving employee performance would significantly improve business results while 73 percent said that their company's most important investment was in people. Still, when asked to rank a number of business priorities, the respondents put performance of people and investment in people near the bottom of the list, well below profitability and other standard measures of performance that are familiar to stock and bond market analysts.[6]

As a result, even in an environment of more rapid economic growth and tighter labor markets, strong public policy interventions will be needed to widely promote workplace cooperation. The tight labor market will create the preconditions for such policy initiatives to be considered seriously. But if they are not implemented when the labor market is tight, sustaining a rising-wage, high-productivity, full-employment economy will be much more difficult.

*   *   *

The policy agenda we have sketched in this chapter moves us well beyond the municipal living wage programs that are the focus of this book. We believe that such wide-ranging changes are needed to achieve and sustain a living wage minimum for all workers in the country. But are we then suggesting that municipal living wage policies themselves can play only a small role in attaining the desired end—the abolition of low-wage poverty in the United States?

Through their direct impact as well as their "ripple effects" on wages and benefits within the affected firms, most municipal living wage laws will contribute only modestly toward eliminating low-wage poverty. But the importance of these laws far exceeds their immediate measurable impact. In dozens of cities, living wage movements have succeeded in dramatizing the issue of low-wage poverty in a way that may be unprecedented over the past twenty-five years in which average real wages as well as the minimum wage have been declining. Moreover, living wage movements have emerged in virtually every region of the country, and through community organizations, religious groups, and local labor movements, not just among full-time policy makers and lobbyists in Washington or the various state capitals. Over time, such local-level organizing initiatives will have far greater staying power than efforts directly primarily at high-level policy makers. Policies must change at these higher levels as well for a living wage minimum to become a national standard. But the local living wage movements are generating a momentum that can't readily be attained at the state or national levels, where the power of big-money politics is far more pronounced.

Indeed, the great merit of municipal living wage campaigns is that they have a realistic chance of winning passage in a large number of communities in the existing political climate. In fact, as we have seen, they have already become law in Baltimore; Milwaukee; Los Angeles; Boston; Portland, Oregon, and several other cities. These measures are becoming part of the country's political and economic fabric. As an increasing number of cities gain experience with these ordinances over the next several years, the limitations of such ordinances as well as their strengths will become evident. This process of political and economic education will then provide a stronghold on which to launch more ambitious programs of egalitarian wage and employment policies, and thus to build a lasting foundation for social and economic justice in this country.

Appendix I–
Suggestions for Researching
Living Wage Prosposals

To estimate the economic impact of a living wage ordinance proposed in your city, you should start by determining the number and types of employers who would be covered by such an ordinance. This can be difficult, as cities do not always keep comprehensive and consistent records on contracts and subsidies. We created our database of firms with the assistance of City Council member Jackie Goldberg's office, which collected a list of most city contracts from Los Angeles city departments for the fiscal year 1995–1996. We supplemented this by writing to all departments for information on financial assistance recipients and concessionaires. As a last resort, we wrote formal requests called California Public Records Act Requests, the state equivalent to Freedom of Information Act Requests. You may want to consider obtaining copies of the actual contracts, so that you get more information, such as the full name and address of the contractor, as well as the exact terms. However, in a large city with hundreds of contracts, this may not be feasible.

Be sure to be specific about what you are requesting, as this can save time. For example, most living wage ordinances cover *service* contracts but not *goods* contracts, so you may get information more quickly if you define your request clearly. However, keep in mind that the details of the ordinance are likely to change during the legislative process. It is therefore important that, within your given time and resource constraints, you get sufficient information so that you can respond readily as details of the ordinance evolve.

Records on service contractors are generally the easiest to obtain. Almost all departments are likely to have at least some service contracts, and in most cases, all contracts must be approved by the city council, so public records are kept on these firms. Money spent on contracts should appear in the city budget (though not always clearly marked as such).

Information on concessionaires can be harder to track down, as these can range from huge operations, such as food and beverage sales at the sports arena, to a one-person hot-dog stand at a city park. Be sure to work with the legal team writing the living wage ordinance in order to figure out which of these concessionaires would be covered. This can be complicated, as concessionaires have different legal arrangements. Some pay a flat monthly fee for the use of the space (e.g., a hot-dog vendor who pays $100 per month to have a cart in a city park). Some pay rent by the square foot (e.g., a boat-repair shop that pays for warehouse space at the harbor). Still others pay a fixed percentage of their gross receipts to the city (e.g., a fast-food restaurant that pays 1 percent of gross receipts for its venue at the airport). The ordinances may not cover all of these arrangements, so be clear on what you are searching for. Then find out which public areas are owned by the city, such as the airports, parks, convention center, harbor, or zoo, and file public records requests to those entities to find out who operates their concessions.

Information on subsidy recipients is the most difficult to find. In some cases, privacy laws prevent city officials from giving out the names of firms that receive special subsidies or tax abatements. In other cases, such as with enterprise zones, programs are administered and records are kept at the state level and not by the cities. Tax-abatement programs do not always show up in city budgets, so you may have to do a lot of work just to determine which programs exist. Again, be specific in order to save time, as many subsidies are not for economic development or job creation, and therefore might not be covered by the ordinance. These may include subsidies for environmental upgrading, assistance for infrastructural repairs after natural disasters, cultural grants, or subsidized loans to homeowners. Again, check with the legal staff to determine which programs would be covered. Some to consider include: enterprise zone reduced-utility-rate programs, Job Training and Partnership Act (JTPA) funds, tax-incremental financing (TIF) districts, industrial revenue bonds, Business Improvement District subsidized loans, and enterprise or empowerment zone tax abatements.

Once you know which firms are affected under the proposed ordinance, you will then be able to find out more about them, such as the wages they pay, the benefits they provide, and the number of low-wage workers they employ. You have several options for getting this information. First, you could conduct a survey. After you have determined the total number of affected firms, you need to decide how many firms you can survey (depending on your time and budget constraints). In small cities you can survey all the firms, but in larger cities with a lot of contractors you will probably need to draw a sample.

Designing survey questions can be difficult, so be sure of what information you want before you begin. A copy of the survey instrument used by the City of Portland is included below.

Surveys can provide useful information, as the figures come directly from the firms and can offer more precision than using estimates from secondary sources. However, surveys can also be expensive and time-consuming, and return rates are often low, especially for mail questionnaires soliciting data on personnel. The average response rate for mail surveys is often less than 50 percent. A letter from a public official, such as the mayor or a city council member, encouraging firms to cooperate with the survey, may improve the response rate. However, even with follow-up phone calls or site visits, it is possible that the return rate would not be high, as firms are often reluctant to provide information about their internal operations.

More importantly, given the nature of the topic, respondents may have an incentive to provide inaccurate responses. For example, it may be in a CEO's interest to state that he or she would consider leaving the region if the city began placing requirements on subsidies, even if such a move were unlikely, or to overstate their number of affected workers in the hope of inflating cost estimates and thereby dissuading public officials from passing the ordinance. While survey data would be an ideal way to answer some of the proposed research questions, the only option to verify the validity of the responses is through on-site observation, or access to company records—both of which are unlikely to be granted, as well as impractical for time and resource reasons in many cases.

Another option to gathering useful data for your campaign is to arrange in-depth interviews with selected employers. In-depth interviews can still be time-consuming, but generally, they are conducted with a much smaller subset than a survey. These interviews can provide more information about employer's attitudes towards topics such as costs and benefits to doing business in the area, factors important to the firm for business location, and the relationship between wage rates and working conditions. These interviews can provide useful anecdotal information that can be used to supplement other research, as well as for potentially locating employers who will act as advocates for the campaign. Usually, employers are not selected randomly, as they would be for a survey sample. Instead, you should take care to select firms with different characteristics, such as a firm that pays high wages, a firm that pays low wages, a manufacturer, a service provider, a small firm, and a large firm, in order to cover a variety of firm types.

Surveys or in-depth interviews with workers can also provide useful information on the relationship between wages and working conditions in contracting firms or in firms that receive subsidies. This information is crucial in the early stages of a living wage campaign, when proponents are crafting the content of the ordinance. It is important to know the current wage level and benefit package received by workers, and if there are particular concerns that should be addressed (such as including subcontractors in the ordinance). These interviews may also provide the personal stories that can show the city council and the press that there are real people behind the broader statistical pictures showing the impact of living wage ordinances.

Finally, a cost-effective and comprehensive alternative to collecting information on firms is the methodology on which we primarily relied. Rather than gathering data directly from firms, we assigned industry codes to each firm (called Standard Industrial Classification, or SICs), in order to attach industry-level statistics, such as the total employment, average wages, and proportion of workforce earning below the living wage rate, to each firm.

The SIC coding system comes from the U.S. Bureau of the Census. You can obtain a copy of the code book from the Government Printing Office or from most larger libraries. The code book was last revised in 1987. SIC codes can be used at the one-digit level to signify the major industry group in which the firm operates (i.e. agriculture; mining; construction; manufacturing; transportation, communication and public utilities; wholesale trade; retail trade; finance, insurance, and real estate; services; and public administration). Beyond that, firms can be classified with greater detail at a two-, three-, or four-digit level. In general, the more precision you use the better, as labor market characteristics can differ greatly by industry. However, four-digit-level information is often not available, so three- or two-digit-level codes must sometimes be used.

SICs can be assigned using commercial sources, such as Dun and Bradstreet listings. This is a listing of about 10 million companies in the U.S., including SIC codes to six digits. However, the Dun and Bradstreet lists are expensive (approximately $900 for the current version) and not comprehensive. A more cost-effective alternative is a software package called Pro-CD Phone Book Plus, which includes addresses and phone numbers, as well as SIC codes for many U.S. businesses. Pro-CD Phone Book Plus can be purchased at major software retailers for less than $200. Be sure to get the version that includes SIC codes.

Industry statistics are available from a variety of government sources. The data we used is described in detail in appendix 3. From these sources, you can obtain the following at the industry level:

1. total number of employees in each of the affected firms;
2. proportion of those employees who earn less than the living wage;
3. average wage earned by those low-wage workers;
4. average wage of all workers in the affected firms;
5. average hours worked by low-wage employees in those firms;
6. average hours worked by all employees in those firms;
7. proportion of low-wage workers who do not have health insurance;
8. proportion of low-wage workers who do not receive paid days off.

With this data, you can then *estimate* the following:

1. the total number of workers that would be affected by the ordinance;
2. full-time equivalent workers affected by the ordinance;
3. the amount of the average wage increase for workers;
4. the total cost of wage increases;
5. the total cost health benefits;
6. the total cost of paid days off.

USEFUL RESOURCES FOR RESEARCHERS

ACORN (Association for Community Organization and Reform Now!). Chapters nationwide; National office in Washington, D.C. (202-547-2500). Provides a packet of materials relating to living wage campaigns, and maintains a current list of where living wage and corporate accountability campaigns are underway. Web site: http://www.igc.apc.org/community/

AFSCME (American Federation of State, County and Municipal Employees) The research office is in Washington, D.C. (202-429-1215). To find out contacts for your area, you can call the national office. Their Web page has useful anecdotal information on contracting out. Web site: http://www.afscme.org

The Corporate Accountability Project. This Web site, sponsored by the EnviroLink Network (412-683-640), has a variety of materials about businesses that may hold contracts or receive subsidies in your area. The site includes the Corporate Welfare Information Center. Web site: http://www.envirolink.org/issues/corporate/index.html

The Economic Policy Institute, Washington, DC (202-331-5510). EPI has produced a variety of useful reports on minimum wages and other labor market topics. Web site: http://epinet.org/

The Los Angeles Living Wage Coalition (213-486-9880) will provide a packet of materials for organizations interested in running their own campaigns.

Minnesota Alliance for Progressive Action, St. Paul, Minnesota (612-641-4050). Their publication, *1996 Corporate Welfare Handbook,* provides useful tips to doing research in your area.

The New Party. Chapters nationwide; National office in New York, New York (1-800-200-1294). The New Party has been instrumental in starting up many of the living wage campaigns. Part of their web page is dedicated specifically to living wage campaigns, and contains useful materials and contact numbers for campaigns around the country. The Web page is located at: http://www.newparty.org

The Preamble Collaborative, Washington, D.C. (202-265-3263). Mark Weisbrot and Michelle Sforza-Roderick of the Preamble Collaborative wrote the 1996 report we discuss, analyzing the Baltimore ordinance: "Baltimore's Living Wage Law: An Analysis of the Fiscal and Economic Costs of Baltimore City Ordinance 442." The Preamble Collaborative has continued to monitor developments in the living wage movement. Web site: http://www.rtk.net/preamble/

SURVEY QUESTIONAIRE TO CITY CONTRACTORS ON WAGES AND HEALTH INSURANCE CITY OF PORTLAND, OREGON, 1995

The following questionnaire was sent to businesses holding contracts with the City of Portland, Oregon, by Gretchen Miller Kafoury, a city council member in Portland at the time. This letter should provide useful guidelines should researchers in other cities seek to gather information via the survey method.

I. Wage Information

Please respond to the following questions:

1) What is the total number of people (or FTE) you employ?
   Full-time: _____   Part-time: _____

2) What is the number of employees paid by your City contract?
   Full-time: _____   Part-time: _____

3) Do any of the employees *paid by your city contract* earn less than $10.00 per hour?   Full-time: _____   Part-time: _____

4) If you answered yes to question 3, please list the job title, number of employees, hourly wage, and estimated total hours worked annually for each position earning less than $10.00 per hour:

Job Title	Number of employees (or FTE)	Hourly Wage Rate	Estimated Annual Hours*

* Please estimate total hours for all employees at this wage.

5) If you were to increase wages for all employees not paid by a city contract to meet a $6.75 wage standard, what would the annual financial impact be on your organization or company?

II. Health Insurance Information

6) Annual employee turnover rate: _____%

7) Average employee length of service with your compamy: _____ years

8) Do you provide employee health insurance?
   Yes _____   No _____

   Any limitations? (e.g., full-time employees only, nintey-day eligibility waiting period, etc.)

9) Do you provide health insurance to dependents or family members?
   Yes _____   No _____

   Any limitations? (e.g., spouse only, paid by employee, etc.)

10) Percentage of monthly premium that is employer paid _____%
    Percentage of monthly premium that is employee paid _____%

11) Percentage of eligible employees enrolled in your health plan _____%

12 Do you offer a flexible/cafeteria benefit plan (Internal Revenue Code Section 125)?
   Yes _____   No _____

13) Medical Plan Information:

   Amount of deductible: $ _____ per year
   Co-payment or co-insurance levels $ _____ or _____%
   Name of insurance provider:
   Name and phone number of broker or contact person for this plan:

Please provide us a copy of your benefit plan booklet with your response to our survey.

Appendix II—
Living Wage and Similar
Measures in the United
States, 1989–97

his is a catalog of the living wage proposals that
have been advanced throughout the United
States between 1989 and 1997. We have sought
to be comprehensive, but inevitably have left out some
proposals. Nevertheless, the information here should
provide a good sense of the range of recent living
wage movements, both in terms of geographic diver-
sity and the variety of proposals either under consideration, passed into law, or defeated.

Living Wage Campaigns, Legislative, Cities

Location	Title	Status	Provisions
Baltimore, Maryland	City Living Wage Ordinance	Enacted December 1994.	Service and professional service contractors required to pay $6.10 an hour in fiscal year 1996; $6.60 an hour in fiscal year 97; $7.10 an hour in fiscal year 98; $7.70 an hour in fiscal year 99, subject to Board of Estimates approval.
Boston, Massachuetts	–	Passed July 1997.	City agencies, service contractors and subsidy recipients (of more than $100,000) must pay $7.49 an hour; Provisions for local hiring, community advisory board on city assistance. Strong monitoring provision.

Location	Title	Status	Provisions
Buffalo, New York	Living Wage Campaign	City Council passed a resolution (September 30, 1997) calling on the city's corporation counsel to draft a bill.	City contractors and subcontractors required to pay minimum of $8.50 an hour to all employees.
Chicago, Illinois	Chicago Jobs and Living Wage Ordinance	Defeated July 30, 1997. (31–17 vote in city council).	Covered service contractors and subsidized businesses required to pay minimum of $7.60 an hour. Provisions for community hiring.
Duluth, Minnesota	–	Passed 1997. (5–4 city council vote).	Firms that receive more than $25,000 in grants, low-interest loans, or other direct aid. Some exemptions. 90 percent of employees must be paid $6.50 an hour with health benefits, or $7.25 without, indexed to inflation.
Durham, North Carolina	–	Ongoing. Passed the Finance Committee.	Businesses with service contracts would be required to pay a minimum wage of $7.55 an hour.
Jersey City, New Jersey	City Ordinance No. 96-063	Enacted June 1996.	Businesses contracting with city for clerical, food service, janitorial and unarmed security services must pay $7.50 an hour; Vacation and health benefits for full-time workers performing contract services.

Location	Title	Status	Provisions
Los Angeles, California	Los Angeles Living Wage Proposal	Passed March 1997. Vetoed by Mayor Riordan, but council overrode veto.	Requires service contractors (more than $25,000) and longer than 3 months), concession-aires, and subsidy recipients (over $1 million or $100,000 ongoing) and subcontractors to pay $7.25 an hour with health benefits or $8.50 without; 12 days paid leave.
Madison, Wisconsin	Living Wage Campaign	Ongoing. City council budgeted $25,000 to cover wage increases.	City contractors required to pay minimum wages at 110 percent of the poverty level and provide health benefits.
Milwaukee, Wisconsin	Living Wage Ordinance	Enacted November 1995.	Requires service con-tractors with contracts greater or equal to $5,000 to pay workers performing contract services hourly wages based on poverty level for family of three. Includes reporting, enforcement, and remedial provisions.
Minneapolis, Minnesota	Recommenda-tions of the Joint Minneapolis–St. Paul Living Wage Task Force.	Passed city council March 7, 1996.	Businesses receiving more than $100,000 a year in financial assistance must pay wages at 100 percent of poverty level for family of four, or 110 percent without health benefits; 60 percent of new jobs created must go to city residents. Prohibits contracting out city jobs for less than living wage.
New Haven, Connecticut	–	Passed July 1997.	Contractors must pay minimum of $7.43 an hour.

Location	Title	Status	Provisions
Pasadena, California	–	living wage ordinance concept approved by mayor and council. Discussion over details is ongoing.	Service contractors (more than $25,000 and longer than 3 months), concessionaires, and subsidy recipients (more than $5,000) and subcontractors. Also covers city agencies and workfare recipients working for the County. $8.50 an hour with health benefits or $11 without.
Pittsburgh, Pennsylvania	"Living Wage" Legislation	Tabled by council (December 1997) after sponsoring member Gene Ricciardi realized he did not have the votes to win.	Employees of city agencies and firms with city contracts or subsidies and city agencies would be entitled to a minimum of $7.73 an hour.
Portland, Oregon	Fair Wages Contracting Ordinance	Enacted May 1996.	City contractors supplying janitors, security guards, parking attendants and temporary clerical workers. $6.75 for fiscal year 96/97; $7.00 fiscal year 97/98; Encourages contractors to purchase health benefits.
Somerville, Massachusetts	–	Ongoing.	Would set a minimum hourly rate of $8.00 for employees of all firms with city contracts of $10,000 or more.
St. Paul, Minnesota	Recommendations of the Joint Minneapolis–St. Paul Living Wage Task Force.	Enacted January 1997.	Businesses receiving more than $100,000 a year in financial assistance must pay wage at 100 percent of poverty level for family of four, or 110 percent ($8.25 an hour) without health benefits; 60 percent of new jobs created must go to city residents.

Location	Title	Status	Provisions
West Hollywood, California	–	Passed unanimously, September 1997.	Service contractors with contracts greater than $25,000 and lasting more than three months must pay $7.25 an hour or $8.50 an hour without health benefits.

Living Wage Campaigns, Legislative, Other Levels

Location	Title	Status	Provisions
Albany County, New York	–	Bill introduced October 20, 1997.	Contractors and subsidy recipients. Includes workfare recipients. $8.55 an hour, plus $0.68 to $1.21 an hour for health benefits for people working more than 15 hours a week.
Dane County, Wisconsin	Living Wage Campaign	Ongoing. County board budgeted $1.25 million to cover wage increases and $300,000 for indirect "ripple effect" costs.	City contractors required to pay minimum wages at 110 percent of the poverty level and provide health benefits.
Maryland State	Living Wage Pilot Program	Announced July 25, 1996. Possible future expansion to other state contracts, depending on results on pilot program.	Contract for cleaning state-owned World Trade Center. $6.60 an hour in 1996 to employees providing service. Rises to $7.10 in 1997; $7.70 in 1998.
Milwaukee County	Living Wage Resolution	Passed May 1997.	Employers of contracted janitors, unarmed security guards, and parking lot attendants required to pay minimum of $6.26 an hour. Rate indexed to prevailing wage. Sets goal of $6.25 an hour for future contracts in other areas.

Location	Title	Status	Provisions
Milwaukee School Board	Livable Wage Resolution	Enacted January 1996.	All public school employees and employees of MPS contractors must pay $7.70 an hour minimum.
Multnomah County, Oregon	–	Passed 1996.	Contractors with higher than average wages, health and other benefits, and neutrality agreements receive preference in contracting.
Orange County, North Carolina	–	Ongoing.	Companies with contracts or financial assistance would be required to pay a living wage (rate not determined yet).

Living Wage Campaigns, Ballot Initiatives

Location	Title	Status	Provisions
St. Louis, Missouri	–	Did not qualify for ballot.	All city contractors and those receiving subsidies $6.25 an hour by 1997; $6.50 by 1998; $6.75 by 1999, 15 cents per year thereafter.
St. Paul, Minnesota	–	Defeated November 1995.	Businesses that receive subsidies must pay a minimum of $7.21 an hour.

Minimum Wage Initiative Campaigns

Location	Title	Status	Provisions
Albuquerque, New Mexico	Citywide Minimum Wage Ballot Initiative	Disqualification of signatures before making it to December 1996 ballot. Legal challenge underway.	Establish city minimum wage at $6.50.
Arizona	Arizona Workers Bill of Rights	Did not qualify for ballot.	Would raise minimum wage to 50 percent of the average family income. Other rights and benefits to workers included.

Location	Title	Status	Provisions
California	Statewide Minimum Wage Ballot Initiative; Proposition 210	Passed in November 1996 general election. 62 percent in favor, 38 percent against.	Raise state minimum wage to $5.00 an hour on March 1, 1997; $5.75 on March 1, 1998.
Denver, Colorado	Citywide Minimum Wage Ballot Initiative; Initiative 100	Defeated in November 1996 general election. 23 percent for; 77 percent against.	Establish city minimum wage at $6.50 an hour on January 1, 1997; $6.85 on January 1,1998; $7.15 on January 1, 1999; annual indexing thereafter.
Houston, Texas	Citywide Minimum Wage Ballot Initiative	Defeated in January 1997 special election. 23 percent for; 77 percent against.	Establish city minimum wage at $6.50 an hour.
Idaho	–	Supporters failed to collect enough signatures to qualify for the November 1996 ballot.	Raise statewide minimum wage to $6.25 an hour.
Missouri	Statewide Minimum Wage Ballot Initiative; Proposition A	Defeated in November 1996 general election. 29 percent for; 71 percent against.	Raise state minimum wage to $6.25 an hour on January 1,1997; $6.50 on January 1,1998; $6.75 on January 1, 1999; 15 cents per year. beginning January 1, 2000.
Montana	Statewide Minimum Wage Ballot Initiative; I-121	Defeated in November 1996 general election. 44 percent in favor, 56 percent against.	Raise state minimum wage to $4.75 an hour on January 1,1997; $5.00 on January 1, 1998; $5.75 on January 1, 1999; $6.25 on January 1, 2000.

Location	Title	Status	Provisions
New Orleans, Louisiana	Citywide Minimum Wage Ballot Initiative for Charter Amendment	Signature gathering completed, but city judge blocked the initiative, citing that it would violate a new state law prohibiting local minimum wage laws.	Establish city minimum wage at $1.00 higher than federal level.
Northampton, Massachusetts	The Job and Living Wage Campaign	Ongoing campaign.	All Hampshire County employers must pay minimum of $7.00 an hour with health benefits, or $8.50 without.
Oregon	Statewide Minimum Wage Ballot Initiative; Ballot Measure 36	Passed in November 1996 general election. 57 percent in favor; 43 percent against.	Raise state minimum wage to $5.50 an hour on January 1, 1997; $6.00 on January 1, 1998; $6.50 on January 1, 1999.
Spokane, Washington	Living Wage Campaign	Ongoing. Supporters are collecting signatures to send to the city council.	All employers who employ workers in the city must pay a minimum wage of $8.25 an hour.
Tucson, Arizona	–	Defeated November 4, 1997.	Would raise minimum wage to $7.00 an hour.

Corporate Accountability Ordinances with Wage or Other Requirements

Location	Title	Status	Provisions
Denver, Colorado	"Corporate Responsibility" Law	Ongoing.	Companies receiving financial assistance must pay $7.70 an hour and target jobs for low- and moderate-income residents.

Location	Title	Status	Provisions
Des Moines, Iowa	–	Passed July 1, 1996.	Recipients of assistance through urban renewal or loan programs. Sets average wage rate goal of $9 an hour (including the value of benefits) for non-management full-time employees.
Gary, Indiana	Ordinance No. 8942	Passed June 22, 1989.	Projects funded by economic development incentive must pay prevailing wages to all employees; health benefits to those working more than 25 hours per week.
Iowa	House File 2180	Passed March 4, 1994.	Wages paid to workers are among factors considered in granting subsidies. The higher the wages paid, the greater the likelihood subsidy will be granted.
Kansas	–	Passed 1990.	Manufacturing firms seeking tax incentives and business assistance must pay better than average wages for state or spend 2 percent of payroll value on training or is certified as participant in state sponsored training programs.
Minnesota	Living Wage Corporate Responsibility Bill	Passed 1995.	Firms receiving $25,000 or more in subsidies must set wage goals and foster job creation within 2 years.
Mississippi	The Mississippi Business Act Program	Passed.	Interest rate on business loans is lowered 0.5 percent for each dollar per hour that the recipient pays its employees above the state's average hourly manufacturing wage.

Location	Title	Status	Provisions
North Carolina	Industrial Redevelopment Bond	Passed	Recipients of IRBs must pay county's average manufacturing wage, or 10 percent above the state average. (Areas of extreme unemployment are exempt).
North Olmstead, Ohio (other cities in Ohio and elsewhere are considering similar measures)	"No Sweatshop" Policy	Passed February 1997.	Prohibits city from buying goods or services produced with child labor or under sweatshop conditions.
San Francisco, California (Los Angeles and New Orleans are considering similar measures)	–	Passed June 1997.	Firms that do business with the city must offer benefits to domestic partners of their employees.
Santa Clara County, California	Manufacturing Personal Property Tax Rebate; Santa Clara County Growth and Job Creation Policy	Passed September 19, 1996.	Tax rebate of property tax levy on manufacturing equipment for businesses locating or expanding within county which pay wages at or above competitive industry wages (at least $10 an hour); provide health care; and meet other conditions.
South Dakota	Senate Bill 118-Section 1	Passed in 1992.	Businesses only eligible for revolving econ. development fund loan unless wage scale for employees begins at no less than $6.10 an hour; at least 85 percent of jobs are full-time; health and other benefits provided.

Location	Title	Status	Provisions
Selected Recent Prevailing Wage Programs, Cities			
New York, New York	City Code Amendment establishing Prevailing Wage Requirement for Certain Service Contracts	Council passed ordinance July 11, 1996; Mayor Giuliani vetoed August 7, 1996; Council overrode veto September 11, 1996.	Requires businesses with certain city contracts for security, temp. office service, cleaning and food services to pay prevailing wages for affected occupations. Rates determined annually by city comptroller, estimated to range between $7.25 and $11.25 an hour.
San Jose, California	Prevailing Wage Ordinance	Enacted 1991.	Amendment to city's little Davis-Bacon act. Requires service contractors with $1,000 or more to pay prevailing wages for work under contract.

Sources:

Worker Options Resource Center, 1997; ACORN; Los Angeles Living Wage Coalition.

Oakes, Larry, "Duluth Council backs ordinance on 'living wage'," *Star Tribune*, July 16, 1997.

Martinez, Michael J. "Albany County Weighs Measure on 'Living Wage'," *The Buffalo News*, October 21, 1997.

Kerstetter, Greg. "Working for a 'Living Wage'," *Daily Hampshire Gazetteer*, February 14, 1997.

"Council to vote on City Wage Hike," *Pittsburgh Post-Gazette*, October 30, 1997.

Martin, Jonathan. "More workers use food bank; High apartment rents, low wages force full-time employees to see free food," *The Spokesman-Review*, October 17, 1997.

Williams, Fred O. "Common Council supports bill calling for 'living wage'," *The Buffalo News*, October 1, 1997.

Himelstein, Linda. "Going beyond city limits?" *Business Week*, July 7, 1997.

Price, Jay, "Living-wage law gets Feb. hearing in Orange," *The News and Observer*, December 4, 1997.

Appendix III— Methodology and Data Sources for Chapter 4

This appendix describes the data sources and methodology used for generating the estimates presented in chapter 4.

DATA SOURCES

ES-202 Unemployment Insurance Data

The ES-202 data are figures collected from all employers who must pay unemployment insurance through the Covered Employment and Wages Program at the Bureau of Labor Statistics (BLS). The laws regarding coverage and the type of information collected vary from state to state, but California has quarterly, universal coverage. Information on the number of establishments, total employment, and total payroll is collected through the State Employment Development Department (EDD) in Sacramento. In other states, the data can be obtained through the BLS or through the state employment agency. Call the BLS at 202-606-6567 or send email to 202_info@oeus.psb. bls.gov to find out the ES-202 contact person for your state.

In most cases, the agency will not release any information on particular firms, but will provide data aggregated by SIC code. For our estimate, we used the 1995 annual average ES-202 data. In order to gain the most industry precision, LA County data was used where three-digit-level SIC information was available, and California state data was used elsewhere.

Current Population Survey (CPS)

The CPS is a national household survey of more than 60,000 households, and includes wage and hour data for all wage-earners in the selected households. We used the 1995 Outgoing Rotation Group merged file to calculate the percentage of workers earning below selected wage rates by industry. The 1995 Annual Demographic (March) File was used to estimate the proportion of low-wage workers who do not have health insurance, and the 1993 National Employee Benefits Supplement was used to estimate the proportion of workers, by wage level, who do not receive paid sick leave. The industry codes used in the CPS do not directly correspond to SICs, but a bridge table is available in the documentation. This bridge converts most codes at the three-digit level, and some at either the four-digit or two-digit level. Data for the LA area was used where sample sizes were large enough. Otherwise, statewide or sometimes national data was used. Some CPS data can be found through the Bureau of Labor Statistics Web site at http://www.bls.gov, but the large datasets are not available on-line and must be ordered through BLS.

IMPLAN

IMPLAN is a software package maintained and sold by the Minnesota IMPLAN Group (MIG Incorporated). The program constructs regional input-output accounts and models, based on a model developed by the U.S. Department of Agriculture. The model uses Census data at the county level and national technical coefficients from the 1982 U.S. input-output matrix to perform regional impact analysis for 528 industries. As with the CPS, the IMPLAN industry codes must be converted to SICs. The IMPLAN documentation provides a bridge table for this purpose.

IMPLAN can generate multipliers for employment, value added, output, personal income, and total income. For this study, we used the input-output tables coupled with the sectoral input expenditures to estimate the number of subcontractors and subcontracted employees. We also used the accounts to derive estimates for firm output. MIG can be reached at 612-439-4421, or by e-mail at implan@mig-inc.com. To review their products, visit their Web site at http://www.MIG-Inc.com.

CALCULATIONS

1. Number of affected workers.

Average employment per firm was estimated from the ES-202 data.

AVGEMP = Total employment/Total establishments, by SIC.

In cases where we knew the actual employment in a particular firm, we substituted in that data for the ES-202 data. This firm-specific data came from details on contracts provided by concessionaires at the airports and from information collected by the Los Angeles Living Wage Coalition. In a few cases, where we knew the employment for particular firms to be larger than the state average (such as food and beverage establishments at the Sports Arena and Coliseum), we made estimates of employment based on specific firm data gathered from similar employers at similar establishments.

To determine how many workers per firm, on average, are paid less than $7.25 per hour, we used the CPS. We totaled the number of workers earning less than \$7.25 per hour by SIC, and divided that by the total employment in the industry to get the average percentage of low-wage workers by SIC.

PCT725 = total workers earning less than \$7.25 per hour/all workers, by SIC.

This multiplied by the average employment per firm gave the average number of low-wage workers per firm.

AFFECTED = AVGEMP * PCT725

Then, we summed the number of affected workers per firm to obtain the total number of low-wage workers affected by the ordinance in covered firms. Since many low-wage workers are also part-time workers, we calculated the average hours worked per week by SIC (from the CPS), and used this to convert the total number of affected workers to full-time equivalent (FTE) employees, assuming 2,000 hours worked per year for full-time employees.

FTES = AFFECTED * AVGHOURS/40 * 2,000 hours per year

As the LA ordinance also covers subcontractors, we then estimated the number of employees in subcontracting firms using the IMPLAN software. From IMPLAN it is possible to determine the volume of inputs (in dollars) from various regional industries required to produce a given dollar amount of output in the final goods or service industry (represented by the service contract, subsidy, or concession agreement). As many of these inputs take the form of subcontracted services, we were able to determine the volume of subcontracting given a particular service contract. IMPLAN also allows us to determine what percentage of the subcontracting dollar amount represents labor costs, thereby allowing for a determination of the number of total subcontracted employees, and the total number of affected subcontracted employees.

For example, a $1 million contract with an engineering firm might require subcontracting services from other engineering firms, as well as janitorial and landscaping services, photocopying or printing services, computer support, and architectural consulting. The input-output model tells us how many dollars of regional inputs are required, on average, for these types of subcontracting services in LA County. IMPLAN also tells us how much of this total volume of subcontracting is comprised of employee compensation. This was adjusted downwards to account for the average compensation for fringe benefits included in employee compensation (39 percent, as cited in Wayne Cascio, *Managing Human Resources: Productivity, Quality of Work Life, Profits.* second Ed. New York: McGraw-Hill 1989). Then, using ES-202 data to determine the size of the firm doing the subcontracting and using the CPS data for wage distribution, we calculated the number of workers receiving less than $7.25 per hour per subcontracting industry. The total of number of workers affected through subcontracting was added to the previous total to obtain a final number of workers affected at the less than $7.25 rate.

Number of affected subcontracted workers per *subcontracted firm* =

(Employee compensation * .61)/Average number of employees per firm * percent earning less than $7.25 per hour.

Number of affected subcontracted workers per *contracted firm* =

Σ all affected subcontracted employees for all subcontracts for each firm.

2. Cost of wage increase.

Wage data from the CPS Outgoing Rotation Group File was used to determine the average wage of those low-wage employees working for the firms in the database.

LOWWAGE = average wage received by those earning less than $7.25, by industry;

WAGEINC = direct increase for affected firms (FTES * (7.25 - LOWWAGE) * 2000).

3. Cost of health insurance.

To estimate the additional workers that would be covered up to $8.50 per hour through the health insurance clause, we recalculated the proportion of workers who, on average, earned between $7.25 and $8.50 an hour by industry, multiplying that by the average employment per industry, and then determining the number of subcontractor employees. This was converted to full-time equivalents using the method above. We multiplied the number of workers in each of the wage categories by the percentage in those categories that do not have health insurance to determine the number of workers who would be eligible for coverage (based on the 1995 CPS Annual Demographics File).

PCT1HB = percent of workers in category 1 (earning less than $7.25 per hour) who do not have health insurance;

CAT1HB = number of category 1 FTE workers (earning less than $7.25 per hour) eligible for health benefits (FTES * PCT1HB):

PCT2HB = percent of workers in category 2 (earning $7.25 to $8.49 per hour) who do not have health insurance;

PCT850 = proportion of workers earning less than $8.50 per hour;

CAT2HB = number of full-time equivalent category 2 workers (earning $7.25 to $8.49 per hour) eligible for health benefits [((AVGEMP * PCT850) * (AVGHRS/40) - FTES) * PCT2HB];

HBCOST = annual cost of health benefits, per firm ((CAT1HB + CAT2HB) * $1.25) * 2000).

4. Cost of mandated paid days off.

In the Los Angeles ordinance, all employees of the covered firm (not just low-wage ones) are eligible for 12 paid days off per year. We estimated the cost of the days off by multiplying the percentage of low-wage workers who currently do not receive paid days off by their average wage, by the number of hours in a work-day, and by the number of mandated days off. The calculation was repeated for higher-wage employees, using a different average wage and proportion of workers currently receiving paid days off. The proportion of workers who do not receive paid days off was estimated using paid sick leave. This comes from the Current Population Survey Employee Benefits Survey.

PCT1DO = percentage of workers in category 1 (earning less than $7.25 per hour) who do not receive paid sick leave;

CAT1DO = number of category 1 FTE workers (earning less than $7.25 per hour) eligible for paid days off (FTES * PCT1DO);

PCT2DO = percentage of workers in category 2 (earning $7.25 per hour or more) who do not receive paid sick leave;

CAT2DO = number of category 2 workers (earning $7.25 per hour or more) eligible for paid days off [((AVGEMP * PCT850) * (AVGHRS/40) - FTES) * PCT2DO];

HIGHWAGE = average hourly wage for workers earning $7.25 per hour or more;

DOCOST = annual cost of health benefits, per firm [(($CAT1DO$ * $7.25)+ ($CAT2HB$ * HIGHWAGE) * 8 hours per day * 12 days per year].

5. Total direct cost to firms.

In addition to the wage and benefit costs, firms will also face other direct costs: payroll taxes and insurance, and compliance costs. The estimates for these are outlined in chapter 4.

PYRLTX = payroll tax (social security) for wage increase, per firm (WAGEINC * 7.65%);

FEDUI = Federal unemployment insurance (WAGEINC * .08%);

STATEUI = State unemployment insurance (WAGEINC * 3.4%);

STATEDIS= State disability (WAGEINC * .01%);

COMPLY = compliance costs, per firm;

DIRCOST = total direct costs, all firms (ΣWAGEINC + ΣHCBOST + ΣDOCOST + ΣPYRLTX + ΣFEDUI + ΣSTATEUI + ΣSTATEDIS + ΣWORKCOMP + ΣCOMPLY).

6. Indirect costs.

The primary indirect cost of the ordinance for firms is what is referred to in the text as the "wage contour"— wage increases given to workers earning above the living wage. The calculations for these are described in chapter 4.

INDCOST = Average cost of wage contour effect.

7. Relative costs for firms.

We summed the direct and indirect costs to obtain the total costs for firms. To see the significance of these costs, we compared them to total output for the affected firms.

Output was estimated in such a way as to adjust for firm size, as we know that some of the firms in the database are much larger than average. We first calculated the annual wages paid to all workers in the firms in our database. This adjusts for firm size as our employment variable CAEMP was manually adjusted for those firms where we knew the actual employment figures.

AVWAGE = average wage for all workers, by industry;

AVHRALL = average hours worked per week, all workers, by industry;

TOTWAGES = [(AVGEMP * AVGHRALL/40) * AVGWAGE * 2,000 hours per year].

We then totaled employee compensation to output by industry (both obtained from Census data, which is available through IMPLAN) to produce an estimate of the average ratio spent on employee compensation per firm, by industry. Since employee compensation includes fringe benefits, we reduced the compensation figure by the average proportion paid in fringe benefits to get a ratio of wages to output.

EC = total employee compensation for industry, LA County;

ECRATIO = ratio of employee compensation to output, adjusted for an average 39 percent fringe benefits (EC(EC*.39)/OUTPUT);

Output was then calculated by dividing the total wages by the ratio of wages to output.

OUT = estimate 2 of average output per firm (TOTWAGES/ECRATIO).

We then divide the total cost of the ordinance (direct costs plus indirect costs) by the different output estimates, to get an estimate of the relative cost (RELCOST) of the ordinance.

RELCOST = (DIRCOST + INDCOST)/OUT.

Appendix IV
Underlying Calculations for Chapter 5 Individual Benefit Figures

The following tables present our calculations for federal and state taxes, food stamps, and Medi-Cal benefits for a family of four with two dependent children. We document our calculations under both Plan Y and Plan Z.

Table A4–1
Plan Y: Federal Income Taxes and FICA Taxes
From 1995 1040 EZ
(1 Full-Time Worker, 2,000 hours of work/year, 1 spouse, 2 dependents)

		Wage = $5.43 hour	Wage = $7.25 hour
1)	*Total wages*	$10,860	$14,500
2)	*Taxable interest income*	$0	$0
3)	*Unemployment compensation*	$0	$0
4)	*1 + 2 + 3*	$10,860	$14,500
5)	*If married enter $11,500*	$11,500	$11,500
6)	*Taxable income (subtract 5 from 4)*	$0	$3,000
7)	*Tax withheld*	$0	$0
8)	*Earned income tax credit*	$3,110	$2,456
9)	*7 + 8*	$3,110	$2,456
10)	*Tax*	$0	$521
11)	*Refund (subtract 10 from 9)*	$3,110	$1,935
12)	*FICA taxes (7.65%)*	$831	$1,109
13)	*Subtract FICA taxes from refund*	$2,279	$826

Table A4–2
Plan Y: State Income Tax and State Disability Insurance
(family of 4, 2,000 hours of work/year)

		Wage = $5.43/hour	Wage = $7.25/hour
1)	*Total wages*	$10,860	$14,500
2)	*Tax* *(1% first $9,662* *2% next $13,236)*	$121	$193
3)	*Credits*	$264	$264
4)	*Income tax paid*	$0	$0
5)	*State disability insurance (0.8%)*	$87	$116
6)	*Total paid to state* *(4 + 5)*	$87	$116

Table A4–3
Plan Y: Monthly Food Stamp Benefits
(1 full-time worker, 2,000 hours of work/year,
1 spouse, 2 dependents over age 6

		Wage = $5.43/hour	Wage = $7.25/hour
1)	*Gross monthly income*	$905	$1,208
2)	*Subtract 20% of gross earned income*	$724	$966
3)	*Subtract $134*	$590	$832
4)	*Subtract dependent care deduction*	$590	$832
5)	*Subtract child support deduction*	$590	$832
6)	*Subtract medical costs for the disabled and elderly*	$590	$832
7)	*Calculate 1/2 of adjusted income*	$295	$416
8)	*Subtract 7 from total shelter costs*	$339	$218
9)	*Subtract 8 from 6 if 8 is < $247. Otherwise, subtract $247.*	$343	$615
10)	*Multiply net income by 30% and round up.*	$103	$184
11)	*Monthly food stamp benefits (subtract 10 10 from maximum allotment for household size)*	$294	$213

Table A4−4
Plan Y: MediCal Benefits
(1 full-time worker, 2,000 hours of work/year,
1 spouse, 2 dependents over age 6)

		Wage = $5.43/hour	Wage = $7.25/hour
1)	Gross monthly income	$905	$1,208
2)	Monthly deductible for children over age 6	$0	$0
3)	Average monthly cost per eligible person (only children are eligible)	$90	$90
4)	Total monthly cost for the coverage of the children (California pays half)	$180	$180

Table A4−5
Plan Z: Federal Income Taxes and FICA Taxes
From 1995 1040 EZ
(1 full-time worker, 2,000 hours of work/year, 1 spouse, 2 dependents)

		Wage = $4.94/hour	Wage = $6.50/hour
1)	Total wages	$9,880	$13,000
2)	Taxable interest income	$0	$0
3)	Unemployment compensation	$0	$0
4)	1 + 2 + 3	$9,880	$13,000
5)	If married enter $11,500	$11,500	$11,500
6)	Taxable income (subtract 5 from 4)	$0	$1,500
7)	Tax withheld	$0	$0
8)	Earned income tax credit	$3,110	$2,760
9)	7 + 8	$3,110	$2,760
10)	Tax	$0	$521
11)	Refund (subtract 10 from 9)	$3,110	$2,239
12)	FICA taxes (7.65%)	$756	$995
13)	Subtract FICA taxes from refund	$2,354	$1,245

Table A4–6
Plan Z: State Income Tax and State Disability Insurance
(family of 4, 2,000 hours of work/year)

		Wage = $4.94/hour	Wage = $6.50/hour
1)	Total wages	$9,880	$13,000
2)	Tax (1% first $9,662 2% next $13,236)	$101	$163
3)	Credits	$264	$264
4)	Income tax paid	$0	$0
5)	State disability insurance (0.8%)	$79	$104
6)	Total paid to state (4 + 5)	$79	$104

Table A4–7
Plan Z: Monthly Food Stamp Benefits
(1 full-time worker, 2,000 hours of work/year,
1 spouse, 2 dependents over age 6)

		Wage = $4.94/hour	Wage = $6.50/hour
1)	Gross monthly income	$823	$1,083
2)	Subtract 20% of gross earned income	$658	$866
3)	Subtract $134	$524	$732
4)	Subtract dependent care deduction	$524	$732
5)	Subtract child support deduction	$524	$732
6)	Subtract medical costs for the disabled and elderly	$524	$732
7)	Calculate 1/2 adjusted income	$262	$366
8)	Subtract 7 from total shelter costs	$372	$268
9)	Subtract 8 from 6 if 8 is < $247. Otherwise, subtract $247.	$277	$485
10)	Multiply net income by 30% and round up.	$83	$146
11)	Monthly food stamp benefits (subtract 10 from maximum allotment for household)	$314	$251

Table A4 – 8
Plan Z: MediCal Benefits
(1 full-time worker, 2,000 hours of work/year,
1 spouse, 2 dependents over age 6)

		Wage = $4.94/hour	Wage = $6.50/hour
1)	*Gross monthly income*	$823	$1,083
2)	*Monthly deductible for children over age 6*	$0	$0
3)	*Average monthly cost per eligible person (only children are eligible)*	$90	$90
4)	*Total monthly cost for the coverage of the children (California pays half)*	$180	$180

—Notes

CHAPTER 1

1. Robert Kuttner, "The 'Living Wage' Movement," *Washington Post*, August 18, 1997.
2. Prof. Tilly's figures are from "Workfare's Impact on the New York City Labor Market: Lower Wages and Worker Displacement," unpublished manuscript, Russell Sage Foundation, March 21, 1996. The *Business Week* story is by Aaron Bernstein, "Off Welfare—and Worse Off," December 22, 1997, p. 38.
3. Stephanie Luce interviewed both Madeline Janis-Aparicio and Tammy Johnson for this book.
4. Frederick H. Borsch, Leonard I. Beerman, and Roy I. Sano, "Should Los Angeles Pass a 'Living Wage' Ordinance? Yes: It Makes Ethical and Economic Sense," *Los Angeles Times*, December 30, 1996, p. B5.
5. Stephanie Luce interviewed Mary Jo Paque. Information on Duluth, Minnesota is from *Star Tribune*, 7/16/97.

CHAPTER 2

1. Even the national minimum wage laws do not apply to all workers. Exemptions are made for trainees and workers in some selected industries including, for example, businesses that do not engage in interstate commerce. As of 1995, approximately 3.7 million workers were paid less than the national minimum wage. The U.S. Department of Labor's *Handy Reference Guide to the Fair Labor Standards Act* (Washington, D.C.: Government Printing Office, 1994), explains the conditions under which firms may be exempt from the national minimum wage law.
2. Lawrence Glickman, *A Living Wage: American Workers and the Making of Consumer Society* (Ithaca, NY: Cornell University Press, 1997), p. 66.
3. John A. Ryan, *A Living Wage: Its Ethical and Economic Aspects* (New York: The Macmillan Company, 1906). Sar A. Levitan and Richard S. Belous, *More Than Subsistence: Minimum Wages for the Working Poor* (Baltimore: The Johns Hopkins University Press, 1979), p. 30.
4. The distinction between "supply" and "service" is not always clear. In the past, the Department of Labor (DOL) has tended to treat some contracts as two separate contracts. For example, a contractor that supplies a photocopier machine and also services that machine may be considered to hold one supply contract and one service contract. The DOL would then make a determination as to the "principal purpose" of the contract, in order to establish which regulation would apply.
5. Jared Bernstein, "America's Well-Targeted Raise," *Economic Policy Institute Issue Brief #118*, September 2, 1997.

6. This calculation is based on the November 1997 figure for the Consumer Price Index of 161.5. We should note here that the official national poverty thresholds established by the U.S. Census Bureau are adjusted annually according to changes in the Consumer Price Index for Urban Consumers, the CPI-U. The reliability of this price index has long been a subject of contention, especially so in recent years (see, for example, Dean Baker, *Getting Prices Right* [Armonk, NY: M.E. Sharpe, 1998] and Robert Pollin, Michael Stone, and Jocelyn Hammaker, "The Illusion of an Improved CPI," *Challenge*, January–February 1991, pp.53–57.). The levels of poverty (though not changes in poverty rate), as well as the real value of the minimum wage, would change somewhat if an alternative price index were used for calculating inflation. However, this is not the place to examine the reliability of the CPI-U. In any case, for what we are trying to measure here—the real level of the minimum wage and poverty thresholds—our view is that the CPI-U is as reliable an index as any possible available alternative.

7. *Myth and Measurement: The New Economics of the Minimum Wage* (Princeton, NJ: Princeton University Press, 1995). David Neumark and William Wascher have criticized the Card and Krueger findings and have produced results of their own which seemed to contradict those of Card and Krueger. However, upon reexamination, the overall thrust of even the Neumark and Wascher results turns out to be supportive of Card and Krueger's findings. This became apparent even though, unlike Card and Krueger, Neumark and Wascher relied to a substantial degree on data provided to them by the Employment Policies Institute, the leading employers group opposing the minimum wage. See John Schmitt's article "Behind the Numbers: Cooked to Order," in the May–June 1996 *American Prospect* for a discussion of the controversy surrounding these different studies.

8. These experiences are succinctly reviewed in William Spriggs and John Schmitt, "The Minimum Wage," in Todd Schafer and Jeff Faux, eds., *Reclaiming Prosperity: A Blueprint for Progressive Economic Reform* (Armonk, NY: M.E. Sharpe, 1996), pp. 163–73.

9. Probably the most comprehensive work by Prof. Peter Phillips and colleagues is the unpublished manuscript, "Losing Ground: Lessons from the Repeal of Nine 'Little Davis-Bacon' Acts (Department of Economics, University of Utah, 1995). This paper, co-authored with Garth Mangum, Norm Waitzman, and Anne Yeagle, includes references to several of their other technical papers and to the broader literature.

10. It has long been charged that Davis-Bacon laws discriminate against minority workers. However, Phillips and his University of Utah colleagues found that minority representation in construction apprenticeship programs fell significantly—from 19.4 percent to 12.5 percent—after little Davis-Bacon laws were repealed (p. 51). More generally, Phillips and colleagues found that the ratio of black-white

unemployment rose after states repealed their little Davis-Bacon laws, which is again contrary to the notion that that black workers have suffered as a result of Davis-Bacon laws (p. 39).

CHAPTER 3

1. *The Rise of the Entrepreneurial State* (Madison: University of Wisconsin Press, 1988), p. xv.
2. Some evidence of the impact of various types of free market restructuring progams is presented in Robert Pollin and Alexander Cockburn, "Capitalism and its Specters: The World, The Free Market and The Left," *The Nation*, February 25, 1991, pp. 224–36.
3. Greg Leroy, *No More Candy Stores: States and Cities Making Job Subsidies Accountable* (Chicago: Federation for Industrial Retention and Renewal; and Washington, D.C.: Grassroots Policy Project, 1994), pp. 144–45. The term "accelerated depreciation" refers to the granting to a company the privilege to deduct from their tax obligations the depreciation of the company's physical plant and equipment at a faster rate than the tax laws normally allow.
4. *No More Candy Stores*, p. 141.
5. H. Brinton Milward and Heidi Hosbach Newman, "State Incentive Packages and the Industrial Location Decision," *Economic Development Quarterly*, August 1989, pp. 203–22. The figures for the BMW and Mercedes-Benz projects come from William Schweke, Carl Rist, and Brian Dabson, *Bidding for Business: Are Cities and States Selling Themselves Short?* (Washington, D.C.: Corporation for Enterprise Development, 1994), p. 23.
6. Michael Wasylenko, "Taxation and Economic Development: The State of the Economic Literature," *New England Economic Review*, March–April 1997, pp. 37–52. The Wasylenko paper is part of the proceedings of a symposium sponsored by the Federal Reserve Bank of Boston on "The Effects of State and Local Public Policies on Economic Development"; the *New England Economic Review* is the research outlet for the Federal Reserve Bank of Boston. The symposium includes contributions by many leading economists working on state and local economic development questions.
7. Wasylenko, op. cit., p. 47, emphasis added.
8. Government Accounting Office, *Industrial Development Bonds: Achievements of Public Benefits Is Unclear*, (Washington, D.C. Government Printing Office, April 1993) p. 18.
9. David E. Dowell, "An Evaluation of California's Enterprise Zone Programs," *Economic Development Quarterly*, November 1996, p, 356.
10. Margaret G. Wilder and Barry M. Rubin, "Rhetoric versus Reality: A Review of Studies on State Enterprise Zone Programs," *Journal of the American Planning Association*, Autumn 1996, pp. 473–91.
11. Peter S. Fisher and Alan H. Peters, "Taxes, Incentives and Competition for Investment," *The Region*, (Minneapolis: Federal Reserve Bank

of Minneapolis, June 1996). This publication is also available on-line through the Federal Reserve Bank of Minneapolis Web site, where we obtained it.

12. The following discussion of Cleveland draws primarily from a June 1996 unpublished manuscript, "Has Cleveland, the "Comeback City", Really Come Back?" by Prof. Norman Krumholz, Department of Urban Planning, Cleveland State University. We are grateful to Professor Krumholz and his assistant Jim Argulante for their efforts in making this work available to us.

13. See, for example, Paul Gottlieb, "Downtown Development Helped Poor," *Cleveland Plain Dealer,* January 18,1997.

14. These figures are reported in Edward S. Herman, "Privatization: Downsizing Government for Principle and Profit," *Dollars and Sense,* March–April 1997, p. 11. See also G. Pascal Zachary, "Two-Edged Sword: More Public Workers Lose Well-Paying Jobs as Outsourcing Grows, *Wall Street Journal,* August 17, 1996, p. A1.

15. Donald F. Kettl, *Sharing Power: Public Governance and Private Markets* (Washington, D.C.: The Brookings Institution, 1993), pp. 160–61.

16. Maryann Mason and Wendy Siegel, *Outsourcing: Thinking Through the Outsourcing Decision* (Chicago: Chicago Institute on Urban Poverty, 1997), p. 5.

17. Herman op. cit., p. 12.

18. Jim Flanagan and Susan Perkins, "Public/Private Competition in the City of Phoenix, Arizona," *Government Finance Review,* June 1995, pp. 7–12.

19. A popular discussion of this policy approach is presented in Joel Rodgers and Dan Luria, *Metro Futures: A High-Wage, Low-Waste, Democratic Development Strategy for America's Cities and Inner Suburbs* (New York: Sustainable America, 1996).

20. Bennett Harrison, Maryellen Kelley, and Jon Gant, "Innovative Firm Behavior and Local Milieu: Exploring the Intersection of Agglomeration, Industrial Organization, and Techological Change," *Economic Geography,* July 1996.

21. Michael E. Porter, "New Strategies for Inner-City Economic Development," *Economic Development Quarterly,* February 1997, pp. 11–27.

22. Ibid, p. 20.

CHAPTER 4

1. Timothy Bartik, a leading authority on the economics of state and local government policies, makes a similar point in discussing survey data, writing that "Another problem with surveys is that businessmen have political incentives to exaggerate the effects of taxes and other economic development incentivesupon their location choices." See his *Who Benefits from State and Local Economic Development Policies* (Kalamazoo, MI: W.E. Upjohn Institute for Employment Research, 1991), p. 27.

2. The logic behind such a calculation follows from our point about indirect "ripple effects" within firms, which we discuss in greater detail below.

3. This effect was first described by the Harvard University labor economist and former Labor Secretary John Dunlop, for example in his book *Wage Determination Under Trade Unions* (New York: A. M. Kelley, 1950); his term for the phenomenon was the "wage contour" effect. David Card and Alan Krueger have more recently described this effect in their pathbreaking book *Myth and Measurement: The New Economics of the Minimum Wage* (Princeton, NJ: Princeton University Press, 1995); they refer to it as the "ripple effect."

4. This recent research is summarized well in William Spriggs and John Schmitt, "The Minimum Wage," in Todd Schafer and Jeff Faux, editors, *Reclaiming Prosperity: A Blueprint for Progressive Economic Reform* (Armonk, NY: M.E. Sharpe, 1996), pp. 167–68.

5. Lawrence Katz and Alan B. Krueger, "The Effect of the Minimum Wage on the Fast Food Industry," *Industrial and Labor Relations Review*, 1992, pp. 6–21.

6. Robert Lacroix and Francois Dussault, "The Spillover Effect of Public-Sector Wage Contracts in Canada," *Review of Economics and Statistics*, 1984, pp. 509–12.

7. The term used by economists for total spending on goods and services is "output," and the technique which has enabled us to estimate these figures is called "input/output" modeling. Appendix 3 briefly describes the IMPLAN regional input/output program which we used in deriving our estimates.

8. The figures for these six high-impact firms were generated through direct industry informtion rather than the government survey data. Details on these estimates are provided in the data appendix.

9. John Rehfuss, *Contracting Out in Government* (San Francisco: Jossey-Bass Publishers, 1989). To say that firms operate in a competitive environment does not mean that they operate in a "perfectly competitive" environment as this term is used in economic theory. That would entail that prices reflect marginal costs and that firms therefore receive no revenues beyond these costs, or what economists term "rents." But the assumption of no rents in municipal contracts—that is, no padding whatsoever in what the firms are able to get from their city contracts—is contrary to the evidence that firms are able to spend heavily on lobbying, entertaining, and bribing city officials in order to win contracts.

10. The profit share (i.e. profits relative to total firm income) estimate, which is described in more detail in the appendix, comes from the same input/output model that we used to estimate total costs. We are not emphasizing these profitability figures, since, unlike our estimates of total costs, the figures for profitability are highly sensitive to the accounting methods one uses to define profits.

11. These calculations assume that workers' productivity does not increase after they receive their living wage increases. Drawing on the

existing evidence that suggests that workers' productivity does rise when their wages and morale are higher, we do raise later in the discussion the possibility of positive productivity benefits from the living wage, though only with respect to firms with a high concentration of low-wage workers.

12. Mark Weisbrot and Michelle Sforza-Roderick, *Baltimore's Living Wage Law: An Analysis of the Fiscal and Economic Costs of Baltimore City Ordinance 442* (Washington, DC: The Preamble Center for Public Policy, 1996).

CHAPTER 5

1. However, the overall benefits for Plans X and Z are not identical. This is first, of course, since Plan Z covers far more workers and firms. But in addition, the average 1995 wage for workers covered under Plan Z, at $4.94, is also lower than the $5.07 average for workers covered by Plan X. This difference in average wages occurs since under Plan Z, we are including the entire Los Angeles low-wage labor market in our data pool, whereas with Plan X, we include only a small subset of that labor market. So even considering just the average individual family, the hourly raise will be 13 cents greater under Plan Z, and that in turn will change overall per-family benefits of the living wage, both for the family itself and for the government.

2. The issue of how creditworthiness is measured among lower-income households, as well as related issues, are developed in Gary Dymski and John Veitch, "Financial Transformation and the Metropolis: Booms, Busts, and Banking in Los Angeles," *Environment and Planning A*, July 1996, pp. 1233–60. A much more extensive treatment of such issues is developed in Prof. Dymski's pathbreaking volume *The Banking Game*, which, as of this writing, is still in manuscript form.

3. As mentioned in Chapter 1, Lawrence Glickman, in his *A Living Wage: American Workers and the Making of Consumer Society*, does explain that the term "living wage" has been used fairly elastically since it was first coined around 1875. However, at no point was the term ever used to describe a wage level so low that a worker could not raise a family above the poverty line. Indeed, Glickman shows the close affinity historically in the usage of the terms "living wage" and "family wage."

4. Douglas Williams and Richard Sander, *An Empirical Analysis of the Proposed Los Angeles Living Wage Ordinance*, Report Prepared Under Contract with the City of Los Angeles, January 1997, p. 61.

5. John Karl Scholtz, "The Earned Income Tax Credit: Participation, Compliance, and Antipoverty Effects," *National Tax Journal*, March 1994, pp. 63–87.

6. Barry Bluestone and Teresa Ghilarducci, "Rewarding Work: Feasible Antipoverty Policy," *The American Prospect*, May–June 1996, pp. 40–46.

7. All the research and the initial drafts of this section were done by our

colleague Prof. David Fairris, in conjunction with our research on the Los Angeles living wage ordinance.

8. William Lazonick's book, *Competitive Advantage on the Shop Floor* (Cambridge, MA: Harvard University Press, 1990) provides an extensive discussion of the Ford Motor experience. Laura Owen presents the most comprehensive analysis of the broader experience of high wage/benefit firms in the early twentieth century in her paper "Worker Turnover in the 1920s: The Role of Changing Employment Policies," *Journal of Economic History*, 55(2), pp. 231–46.

9. Information on Bell Industries is based on company documents and Prof. Fairris's interviews with Theodore Williams and Howard Schwartz, director of human resources.

10. The information on All American Home comes from company documents and a personal interview by Prof. Fairris with Mr. Gertler.

11. The information on Rogers Poultry is based on Prof. Fairris's interview with plant director Terry Carter and company documents.

12. The information on No-Name Meats comes from city documents, the *Los Angeles Times*, and interviews with workers at the firm conducted by associates of the Tourist Industry Development Council.

13. Many such firms, including the Fortune 500 firm Nucor Corporation and Magma Copper in Tuscon, Arizona among the largest, are described in David Gordon, *Fat and Mean: The Corporate Squeeze of Working Americans and the Myth of Managerial "Downsizing"* (New York: The Free Press, 1996), and Eileen Appelbaum and Rosemary Batt, *The New American Workplace: Transforming Work Systems in the United States* (Ithaca, NY: Cornell University ILR Press, 1994).

14. Recent evidence on the union wage premium is presented in Lawrence Mishel, Jared Bernstein, and John Schmitt, *The State of Working America 1996–97* (Armonk, NY: M.E. Sharpe, 1997), pp. 199–200. An extensive, but earlier discussion is H. Gregg Lewis, *Union Relative Wage Effects* (Chicago, IL: University of Chicago Press, 1985).

CHAPTER 6

1. Much of this chapter's subsequent discussion is drawn from Robert Pollin and Elizabeth Zahrt, "Expansionary Policy for Full Employment in the United States: Retrospective on the 1960s and Current Period Prospects," in Jonathan Michie and John Grieve Smith, eds., *Employment and Economic Performance: Jobs, Inflation and Growth* (New York: Oxford University Press, 1997), pp. 36–75.

2. These examples, as well as a more extensive discussion of this question, are found in Robert E. Scott, "Trade: A Strategy for the Twenty-first Century," in Todd Schafer and Jeff Faux, *Reclaiming Prosperity: A Blueprint for Progressive Economic Reform* (Armonk, NY: M.E. Sharpe, 1996), pp. 245–62.

3. This discussion of the effect of the business attack on unions on wages draws from the late David M. Gordon's important last book, *Fat and*

Mean: The Corporate Squeeze of Working Americans and the Myth of Managerial "Downsizing" (New York: The Free Press, 1996), especially chapter 8. The latest figures on unionization rates come from the Bureau of Labor Statistics.

4. Dean Baker, Robert Pollin, and Marc Schaberg, "Main Street vs. Wall Street: Taxing the Big Casino," *The Nation*, May 9, 1994, pp. 622–24.

5. Both Gordon's proposal and that of the Dunlop Commission, as well as a summary of the results of the survey of working people, are summarized in Gordon's *Fat and Mean*, op. cit., p. 243.

6. These figures, as well as a generally illuminating discussion of the issues surrounding the establishment of cooperative workplaces, are presented in Eileen Appelbaum and Peter Berg, "Financial Market Constraints and Business Strategy in the United States," in Jonathan Michie and John Grieve Smith eds., *Creating Industrial Capacity: Towards Full Employment* (Oxford: Oxford University Press, 1996), pp. 192–224. See also Eileen Appelbaum and Rosemary Batt, *The New American Workplace: Transforming Work Systems in the United States* (Ithaca, NY: Cornell ILR Press 1994) and David Gordon, *Fat and Mean* for extensive discussions of these same issues.

—Index